Into Great Freedom

From Purgation to Illumination

By Mark Hartfiel

PARADISUS DEI®
P.O. Box 19127
Houston, TX 77224

www.paradisusdei.org

Dedicated to the men of TMIY and their families.

Cover Design: Fuzati

Table of Contents

Introduction

"Late have I loved you, beauty so old and so new: late have I loved you. And see, you were within and I was in the external world and sought you there, and in my unlovely state I plunged into those lovely created things which you made. You were with me, and I was not with you. The lovely things kept me far from you, though if they did not have their existence in you, they had no existence at all. You called and cried out loud and shattered my deafness. You were radiant and resplendent, you put to flight my blindness. You were fragrant, and I drew in my breath and now pant after you. I tasted you, and I feel but hunger and thirst for you. You touched me, and I am set on fire to attain the peace which is yours" (St. Augustine, Confessions).

This is a journey for souls who thirst to enter into the heart of the Father. It's a desire for liberation out of the wilderness, out of the bondage and trappings of this world. In the Father's heart, there is great freedom. In his love, we find our true selves. By the grace of God, it is time to break free from whatever is holding us back. On our pathway back to the Father we pass through three primary states:

1. **The Purgative State:** Actively working to overcome vices and sins.
2. **The Illuminative State:** Freed from vices and detached from the world, God can reveal his mysteries and illuminate the mind.
3. **The Unitive State:** The state of perfect charity and profound union with God.

Since most souls will not enter into the state of perfect charity and profound union with God until Heaven itself, we will only spend a small portion of our time on the Unitive. Our precise goal for this journey is simple and yet audacious, passing from the Purgative into the Illuminative! Therefore, our aspiration is to provide a pathway and a practical toolbox for those who are willing to try! St. Augustine reminds us that it won't be easy, "Many have tried to return to you, and have not had the strength in themselves to achieve it."

I very much relate to these words from St. Augustine, weak and utterly unable to reach the heights of sanctity on my own will and merits. Thanks be to God, I've learned two secrets for overcoming this wretched condition:

1. Like St. Paul (see 2 Corinthians 12:10), little Therese of Lisieux and countless other saints, embrace your weakness: Don't rely upon your strength but rather lean on the Lord. We can't do this alone!
2. Offer your spiritual practices for others: prayers, mortifications, joys and sufferings. Make it personal. Name names. Your wife, your children, your grandchildren, your parents, your friends, those in most need, etc.

For example, there have been many times when I have personally felt too weak and apathetic to pray the Rosary, until one day it came to mind to offer it for my wife and my children. I started offering each decade for a very specific person by name. When praying a daily Rosary for other people, it was as if God bestowed supernatural grace and strength upon me to faithfully preserve. The same can be true for you. As you walk through this journey, offer it for someone or even a variety of people. How about pulling out a pen and a sheet of paper and writing out 40 names? Each day you can offer this for one of those friends or loved ones. God can and will provide the grace and strength for you to endure.

The greatest gift you could ever give your spouse, children, the Church and this world is your personal holiness. Everything else will pass away. I cannot promise you an easy road ahead, but I can certainly promise you an adventure of a lifetime that will include more joy and satisfaction than anything the world could ever offer you! God cannot be outdone in generosity. Let us invest ourselves in the Lord over these next forty days and trust in his promises.

Filled with gratitude, I want to give credit to two primary sources that helped form my thought and contemplation for this work. First and foremost, Steve Bollman and the That Man is You! (TMIY) men's program. Although I have a theology degree, I can say I have learned more about the spiritual life from Steve and TMIY! than any other single source. My understanding of the three states or "ways" of the spiritual life and the concept of implementing spiritual practices to counteract the flesh, the world and the devil came through conversations with Steve and his deep understanding of spirituality within the Church. I personally believe TMIY is so rich and bountiful in its content that numerous books could be written as an offshoot of the program.

The next person I would like to give credit to is Fr. Dave Pivonka. Fr. Dave has given multiple talks within That Man is You! "The Vision of Man Fully Alive" series that deal exclusively with freedom. He has also written a book titled, "Spiritual Freedom". I didn't fully realize how much his contemplation and work on freedom had influenced my thought until I completed this book. I love how he used the story of Pharaoh and the Israelites to explain authentic freedom, the source of our bondage and God's initiative for our freedom. Those specific themes will emerge within this work. To Fr. Dave, thank you!

I would also like to give a very special thanks to my brother, Matt, a.k.a "Big Hart". His prayerful read and edit has touched every page and nearly every paragraph in some fashion. If you read a beautifully flowing passage somewhere along the way, most certainly you have my brother to thank!

Finally, my initial inspiration to put this together was for the men of TMIY. Although anyone (male or female) at any stage in their walk with the Lord will enjoy and benefit from this journey. Let us all seek the Lord with an earnest heart and desire more of him.

In Christ,
Mark Hartfiel

Forward

The human person is free. Remarkably, God created us that way. It was this way from the beginning; freedom was and is a part of God's plan for you and me. But you have to wonder, if God had the opportunity to do it again, would he have done it that same way? I mean, hasn't our freedom caused lots of problems?

The world would have you believe this: but in fact, most of the world's problems are when we fail to act in freedom. When we are truly operating in freedom things actually go great. It's when we are not free that everything falls off the rails. In the end, freedom is the ability to do what is good, right and holy: it is when we act against this that our bondage is actually revealed.

God gifted us with the grace of freedom. God is totally and radically free and he shared this freedom with us—his creation. It's an understatement that we haven't handled this freedom very well, not in the beginning and certainly not now. But God still desires our freedom and has provided us every grace necessary for us to be free.

In this book, Mark has done a wonderful job at presenting this gift of freedom. His presentation is clear, concise and relevant. He shares personal experiences and stories and draws from the lives of the saints in order to bring clarity and inspiration. I particularly appreciate his approach of a single reflection for forty days. This model, breaking things down in small parts, makes an eternally important topic like freedom more within our reach. It may actually be possible to be free.

And it is. We can be free not because we are so powerful, disciplined or holy; rather, because we are profoundly weak and need the grace of God in order to bring us to freedom. The moment we realize that freedom is not possible by our own strength of character but only through developing a relationship with Christ that is animated by the Holy Spirit, then freedom can become a reality. I encourage you to enter into the journey that will lead from slavery to the Kingdom of God.

Fr. Dave Pivonka, TOR

Section 1:

A Heart on Fire

"Be who God meant you to be and you will set the world on fire."

St. Catherine of Siena

Day 1
A Heart on Fire with Desire

"Teach me to be a saint." Those were the words of the young, bright-eyed Dominic Savio as he met and came to know the great St. John Bosco, affectionately known simply as Don Bosco. The words of a child. The desires of a child. The purity of heart of a child.

In a book dedicated to growing in spiritual maturity, why begin with a statement from a mere child?

Scripture tells us that from the overflow of the heart that the mouth will speak (Matthew 12:34). At the heart of Dominic Savio was a consuming thirst for God and a burning desire for holiness. He longed for nothing less than to be a saint. And as history would tell, Don Bosco instructed Dominic and laid out a pathway to holiness, which Dominic faithfully and humbly fulfilled throughout his life. In fact, he lived it so well that in 1954 Dominic was recognized by the Church as Saint Dominic Savio. He actually became a Saint! A holy desire was fulfilled!

Just like falling in love, the spiritual life begins with desire. As we embark upon this forty-day journey together, we too must long and thirst for something more. What Dominic said to Don Bosco we must cry out today in our hearts, "Lord, teach me to be a saint! Set my heart on fire with desire!"

This desire is born from an encounter with Christ, and since you have picked up and are reading this book, I will assume you have had at least one experience with the living God. So from where we stand today, you are likely either: 1) thirsty for more, or 2) in need of rediscovering that thirst.

Take a moment to pause and reflect upon where you currently are in your spiritual life.

- Are you just beginning the journey after an incredible encounter with the Lord, anxious to know what's next?
- Have you been walking with the Lord for many years, but burned out and seemingly going through the motions?
- Does your heart burn with desire for the Lord and his goodness?

The good news is wherever you are in your spiritual life, Jesus Christ wants to encounter you right there and take you further. If you've ever been to a That Man is You! Men's Program you have heard Steve Bollman boldly proclaim this many times. And he's right! The God who is meek and humble of heart, full of mercy and compassion, yearns to meet you right there where you stand, no matter where that is.

You don't have to be a saint to set out upon this journey with us. "If God counted our iniquities, Lord, who could stand?" (Psalm 130:3). The saint is not the one who doesn't have mess in his or her life; the saint is the one who gives their mess fully to God and allows God into it. It was the saints themselves that taught us that sanctity is in the struggle.

Our pilgrimage ahead will be about entering into this struggle and engaging in the war that exists for our souls, selfishly striving to steal our joy. We will dive into the trenches and attack our fears head on, finding a pathway to holiness amidst the conflict. No longer a far reaching, pie-in-the-sky ideal, the fire for sainthood will begin igniting in our hearts with passion and purpose.

You were made with one purpose: to be a saint! Echoing the words of St. Dominic Savio, "If I am not trying to be a saint, I am doing nothing at all."

Day 2
A World Ablaze

To make substantial spiritual progress, St. Dominic Savio's desire must become our desire. It starts with throwing out the spirit of mediocrity in the spiritual life that seems to pervade the average lay person's thoughts. The devil craves for us to live there, in this sort of complacent, lukewarm place where we are neither hot nor cold, like a race car idling on the track. Our Lord proclaims the opposite, "I came to cast fire upon the earth; and would that it were already kindled!" (Luke 12:49).

Don Bosco didn't try to discourage Dominic Savio's eagerness because of his youth, nor did he withhold the reality of the long, at times difficult, road ahead. Rather, he embraced that desire and ignited it, handing him a burning torch from one heart on fire to another! Don Bosco proceeded to teach Dominic Savio and his other apprentices three fundamental beliefs:

1. It's God's will that each one of you should become a saint.
2. It's easy to become a saint.
3. There is great reward in Heaven for those who try.

Let's ponder each of these more deeply.

It's God's will that each one of you should become a saint.

It is absolutely critical that we understand this universally as well as personally. As we've stated, it's not just his will for you but also his burning desire! If we never grasp this gift and take hold of our inheritance, then by nature something went terribly wrong.

It's easy to become a saint.

Excuse me, come again? Of all the things in life that come to mind as considered "easy", sainthood doesn't usually show up at the top of the list. Diving deeper, Don Bosco tells us:

1. Do ordinary things in an extraordinary way.
2. Accept what the day brings you.

Well, let's give Don Bosco this...those concepts *sound* easy and simple from the standpoint of not being complex. Easy to understand, but not always so easy to live. In fact, sometimes the simplest of things can be the most difficult.

There is great reward in Heaven for those who try.
As we've mentioned, the process may be messy. To be a little more bold in my assertion...the process will be messy. We will rise and fall over and over again. Life will bring about both interior and exterior trials, as we are tempted, pruned, wounded, scourged, heartbroken, and even tormented. But don't get me wrong, this adventure will also be glorious! We will grow closer to God as we come to know and experience his love. Our souls will experience tastes of Heaven even here on earth; our hearts delighting in treasures the world simply cannot offer. Becoming spiritually richer than even the richest man and wiser than any human wisdom, we will develop a peace and joy that "surpasses all understanding" (Phil 4:7). Dominic Savio understood this well as he proclaimed, "I will not have any peace if I don't keep on trying!" Even if we fall short in our honest and sincere attempt to reach heroic sanctity in this life, the reward will be great in Heaven. But it can also be great here on earth!

The Lord patiently waits to enter into your life and take the ordinary things you do and make them extraordinary. "What no eye has seen, nor ear heard, nor the heart of man conceived, what God has prepared for those who love him" (1 Cor 2:9).

This journey is about you. It's about all the love the Father wishes to generously lavish upon you. It's about all the wonderful things the Father wishes to accomplish through you. He will surely pour out extraordinary graces for those who love him, those whose hearts burn with a sincere and humble desire.

Don Bosco challenges us to do ordinary things in an extraordinary way. Over time, new habits are formed and our perspective of the world begins to change. As Pope Pius XI so simply yet profoundly professed, "In Don Bosco, the extraordinary becomes ordinary."

Lord, teach *me* to be a saint.

Section 2:

The Force of Freedom

"Freedom is the power, rooted in reason and will, to act or not to act, to do this or that, and so to perform deliberate actions on one's own responsibility. By free will one shapes one's own life. Human freedom is a force..."

Catechism of the Catholic Church, 1731.

Day 3
The Force of Freedom

And God said, "Let there be light"; and there was light.
Genesis 1:3

Day 1 began with quite possibly the first words St. Dominic Savio spoke to St. Don Bosco; today we begin with God's very first words in all of salvation history. When God speaks, he speaks with force and power! BOOM! An explosion of light lit up the cosmos!

Speaking of light, let's consider our massive sun for a moment. Over a million Earths would fit into the sun, which has a diameter of almost a million miles. As impressive and unique as the sun seems, the Milky Way Galaxy contains an estimated 2 to 3 billion stars just like it!

For the next three paragraphs, I'm going to borrow some information from "The Evidential Power of Beauty", one of many great works by Fr. Thomas Dubay. For example, if you go to the beach and pick up a hand full of sand, ten thousand grains of sand lie within your grasp. Taking all the grains of sand on all the beaches across the entire earth, there would still be more stars in the universe than grains of sand on the face of the Earth. By the breath of his mouth, he spoke them into existence with just a short phrase (see Psalm 147:4). God's Word is a powerful force!

But we're not done considering light just yet! Given light travels at a speed of 186,000 miles/second, it takes a sun ray eight minutes to reach our skin. Putting some of our best technology to work, it would take a jet plane (traveling at 500 mph) 18 years to cover this same distance! Meanwhile, light is busy circling the Earth about seven times a second. Let's say we decided to get a little ambitious and fly our jet plane to the next closest star, Proxima Centauri. At roughly four light years from Earth, the estimated time of arrival would be about 5.5 million years. And for the really adventurous that want to make the trek across the diameter of our galaxy...100,000 million years.

Finally, stepping into the realm of almost incomprehensibility, our "known" universe spans an estimated 12-15 billion light years and continues to grow. Modern science now projects approximately 50 billion galaxies exist in the universe and each of them with potentially 2-4 billion stars. To date, scientists have discovered a star 500 times the size of the sun, and another, with 6.5 million times the brightness of the sun!

As we take a moment to exhale, I dare to say that the vastness of the universe and awesome splendor of God's creation leaves many of us speechless, in complete awe and wonder of all that he has created. These very first words, "Let there be light", suddenly carry with them a dynamic power and mighty force so unimaginable that we are left in complete humility, gasping for air.

Just one chapter later, we read God's first three words ever spoken to man. With this new disposition and appreciation, I leave you to contemplate another simple phrase spoken with that same divine power:

"You are free…" (Gen 2:16).

Day 4
The Pursuit of the Father

"Freedom!!!" I can still hear William Wallace shout this out in the epic Braveheart scene as he awaited his executioner. It sent chills down the spines of millions of viewers who felt that emotion in the depths of their being. This part of the movie was so powerful to all of us; not because deep down we are all Scottish rebels seeking freedom from English oppression, it's because we were all made free from the very beginning!

Unfortunately, this great gift of freedom was abused. We chose (and continue to choose) bondage, and ever since God has been working overtime to try to restore us to freedom. This movie captured our hearts and imaginations because this is our story! Recall the words of Wallace's classic and inspiration rally speech, listening with spiritual ears this time:

"You have come to fight as free men, and free men you are. What would you do without freedom? Will you fight?... And dying in your beds many years from now, would you be willing to trade all the days from this day to that for one chance, just one chance to come back here and tell our enemies that they may take our lives, but they'll never take our freedom!" (Braveheart).

With that, the Scottish men go charging out after their enemy, literally running *into* the battle! This is our battle cry. Through the course of this journey we will identify our enemy and in the name of freedom, engage in the battle. We will confront the enemy.

God created us in his image and likeness, the Imago Dei. You see, God himself is free, and since we are mysteriously made like him, we too must be free! But when we sin, this image is distorted and we lose that freedom. We become less human. Sin, in a word, dehumanizes us. Sin enslaves us.

Even in our sinfulness, God the Father unceasingly loves us as his children, with a patient, potent and permanent pursuit. He became a man like us, died for us, rose for us, sent us his Spirit, and gave (and continues to give) us his live-giving resurrected body as our daily bread. Why such extremes? St. Paul proclaims, "For freedom Christ has set us free" (Galatians 5:1).

Our God goes to great lengths to restore us to freedom and unbind us from the chains of sin. Christ himself exhorts us, "Truly, truly, I say to you, every one who commits sin is a slave to sin" (John 8:34). We will get into this more deeply as we progress, but we don't have to wait until the New Testament to see God's desire in action as we read from the Old Testament:

"Then the Lord said to Moses, "Go in to Pharaoh, and say to him, 'Thus says the Lord..."Let my people go..."(Exodus 9:1).

I want you to stop for a moment to really understand this next statement and take it in deeply: Your freedom is *God's* initiative! This will be a recurring theme in this book and in your life. God will never stop pursuing your freedom. It was his initiative to create you free and it's his initiative to restore you to freedom. Our job is to trust in God, trust in his ways, trust in his goodness, and cooperate and work with him in his plan for our lives. The real issue is trust! This notion that surrendering our lives fully over to God will somehow restrict our freedom, take away our fun and bring us less joy is a straight-up twisted lie. And every single time we sin, we fall into that lie hook-line and sinker:

"Man, tempted by the devil, let his trust in his Creator die in his heart and, abusing his freedom, disobeyed God's command. This is what man's first sin consisted of. All subsequent sin would be disobedience toward God and lack of trust in his goodness" (CCC 397).

God has had a plan to restore our freedom ever since the fall of Adam and Eve, and he has a plan for your freedom today. He has a plan to free you from the source of your bondage, no matter how helpless it may seem. Yes, the Lord used Moses as an instrument for his people's freedom, but it was indeed God taking the lead. Notice God's strategy, his battle plan if you will. He focuses directly on the source of their bondage. "Go in to Pharaoh, and say to him...'Let my people go...'"(Exodus 9:1).

In order for us to be set free, we are going to have to identify and confront the very source of our bondage. We can all relate deeply to this story of Pharaoh and the Israelites. Our daily struggle with the bondage of sin and need for God's goodness and mercy is as relevant today as it was at the time of Moses.

Day 5
A Legitimate Question

The Israelites could clearly see the source of their bondage. He had a name and a face – Pharaoh. It was extremely tangible.

For most of us in the Western World, we do not experience the same type of bondage as the Israelites. Our slavery is not due to an unjust ruler that lords over or binds us. In fact, America boasts of its freedom. We are a country built on individual freedom. We take great pride in being 'the land of the free.' But what does freedom really mean?

In his last book, "Memory and Identity", Saint John Paul II made a bold proposition, "One may legitimately ask whether [the socioeconomic system of the West] is not another form of totalitarianism, subtly concealed..."

Make no mistake, totalitarianism is a strong and very pointed concept and worldview, requiring complete subservience to its masters. It's safe to say John Paul II is questioning our freedom, to say the least. On many occasions, he described the West as "The Culture of Death," which isn't the most endearing endorsement either. His predecessor, Pope Benedict XVI, doubled down labeling the West "a dictatorship of relativism," a worldview denying the existence of objective and absolute morality and truth.

If the truth will set you free, then the lack of absolute truth will certainly do the opposite. Depending upon your definition of freedom, 'the land of the free' evolves into the 'not so free'. Spiritual bondage then evolves into an even deeper bondage than physical bondage, with eternal rather than temporary implications at stake. Bondage of a soul for all eternity is known as hell. Yikes! We started our journey by saying that God's burning desire for you was for your freedom; now Satan's burning desire for you has been revealed. Unfortunately, it's a different kind of fire and I'm not interested in joining the misery of his company.

God cares about both the physical and the spiritual. We saw yesterday that it was undeniably God's initiative to set his people free from the captivity in Egypt. Furthermore, this story from salvation history foreshadowed what was to take place and reach ultimate fulfillment in Jesus Christ. Christ came not just for the Israelites but for the entire world. The new Moses (Jesus) came not merely for a physical freedom of land but a spiritual freedom from the chains of sin. He came to break our chains and set us free!

I've heard it said that when you swim in the ocean you start to smell like fish. Although we live in a beautiful world, meticulously crafted by the hands of God, it also has within it cultural concerns that require daily inner as well as external reflection and discernment to identify sources of bondage and honestly assess how free we really are.

Tomorrow, we take the next step in our journey and begin the process to clearly name our Pharaoh. Once we name it, we will confront it!

Section 3:

Naming Your Pharaoh

"You will never be free until you allow God to address the "pharaoh" in your life...it is better to be on the path to freedom and experience difficulties than to remain a slave in the land of the pharaoh."

Fr. Dave Pivonka, Spiritual Freedom

Day 6
Bless Me Father for I have Sinned

I recently participated in the Sacrament of Reconciliation, beginning my confession in traditional fashion, "In the name of the Father, and of the Son, and of the Holy Spirit. Amen. Bless me Father for I have sinned. My last confession was [insert amount of time]."

But this time my *next* line was different. "My predominant fault is _____." I named it. I confronted it. I called it out. It was the next step in my personal journey towards freedom.

Each one of us has a predominant fault, a weakness within us that tends to be more prevalent than the others. Each person may have a different struggle. One may have intense battles with lust while the other is consumed with greed. Another may struggle with an all-consuming pride on his or her climb up the corporate ladder, while yet another may toil with a vision-less apathy that borders on sloth. It's important to understand that we don't all trod the exact same pathway towards freedom.

"Go in to Pharaoh, and say to him..."Let my people go..."(Exodus 9:1). In a very specific, tangible and personal way, I confronted Pharaoh. I went face-to-face with the deep-seeded source of my bondage. Now don't get me wrong, knowing it and naming it did not instantly grant me outright and efficacious freedom (just ask the Israelites!), but it was a huge step in the right direction. This concept of discovering your predominant fault has been a part of the rich history of spirituality within the Church for centuries. Nonetheless, only recently did I discover the phrase "naming your Pharaoh" in Fr. Dave Pivonka's book "Spiritual Freedom," and absolutely love it!

Now let's take a step back for a moment. There are enemies in the spiritual life and regrettably, we are born with an innate impulse towards them. Newsflash – we bear a tendency and propensity towards sin! It's known as concupiscence, and the more we give into it, the more power it has in our lives. "For all that is in the world, the lust of the flesh and the lust of the eyes and the pride of life, is not of the Father but is of the world" (1 John 2:16).

The flesh, the world and the devil; three areas that give us the most trouble. They are the big three; the three-headed monster so to speak. Properly speaking, these are our greatest enemies because they simultaneously separate us from God, separate us from the desires of our heart and enslave us to sin. While it's true that you and I did not personally choose to receive original sin, we certainly are guilty for choosing to sin through our own free will. We can't just blame Adam and Eve; we have all taken a bite from the forbidden fruit at one time or another.

If you are in a war, you have to know your enemies intimately and with great detail. Identifying who or what you are up against and building a clear and winning strategy is essential to enduring a positive outcome. Does anyone ever win a war by merely playing defense, continually retreating and building up walls while the enemy surrounds you from every direction? While maintaining a defensive stature and position is key, you must also go on the offensive and attack! As we continue the journey, we will learn both offensive and defensive maneuvers, but knowing our enemy must come first. It's mission critical. We shall target the very source of our bondage and then confront it with the same passion and potency as Moses did with Pharaoh.

Imagine knowing the source of your bondage with clarity and then establishing a plan to build strength specifically in that area. What difference would that make? Tomorrow our three enemies will turn to seven (the seven deadly sins) and things will get even more personal. But before we go there, I would like to tell you the second half of my confession story with the good and wise priest.

Father said, "Now I will give you *the secret* to the spiritual life. You must understand these (your sins) as enemies. You must understand you are at war against these enemies. But don't beat yourself up over these. Instead, with Christ, you must fight against them, not against yourself. In order to win a war, a soldier should never go into battle with self-inflicted wounds."

This advice is beyond wise – it's pure gold! Don't allow your sins or your bondage to lead you to lose hope and despair. Despondency is a straight shot from the enemy on the battlefield for your soul. If you know your enemy, have Christ at your side, infused with the desire for authentic freedom and the willpower to fight, you are well on your way to winning the war. The battles won't be easy, but looking back you will reflect upon and find pleasure in the greatest and most fruitful adventure of your life.

"For the creation waits with eager longing for the revealing of the sons of God...because the creation itself will be set free from its bondage to decay and obtain the glorious liberty of the children of God...and not only the creation, but we ourselves ... What then shall we say to this? If God is for us, who is against us? He who did not spare his own Son but gave him up for us all, will he not also give us all things with him?" (Romans 8:19-32)

Day 7
Identifying your Predominate Fault

In this book, we are naming names. It's time. Over the next several days we will grow in understanding of the predominant areas of sinfulness in our lives and thereby come to know the source of our bondage, the "Pharaoh" that seeks to bind us in shackles. For Christ teaches us, "Truly, truly, I say to you, every one who commits sin is a slave to sin" (John 8:34).

Yesterday we met the three-headed monster known as concupiscence. It's the tendency towards sin which we specifically classified in the context of the flesh, the world, and the devil. Today we will learn how the infamous seven deadly sins fit within this predicament.

The Flesh (Deadly Sins 1-4):
1. Lust: A "disordered desire for or inordinate enjoyment of sexual pleasure. Sexual pleasure is morally disordered when sought for itself, isolated from its procreative and unitive purposes" (CCC 2351).
2. Gluttony: The inordinate desire for the pleasure connected with food or drink.
3. Sloth: Sluggishness of soul or boredom because of the exertion necessary for the performance of a good work.
4. Wrath: The desire of vengeance. "If anger reaches the point of a deliberate desire to kill or seriously wound a neighbor, it is gravely against charity; it is a mortal sin" (CCC 2302).

The World (Deadly Sins 5-6):
5. Greed: The inordinate love for riches. Like lust and gluttony, it's a sin of desire. It implies an artificial, controlling passion for wealth or possessions. St. Paul essentially equates greed with idolatry, "Put to death therefore what is earthly in you: immorality, impurity, passion, evil desire, and covetousness, which is idolatry (Colossians 3:5).
6. Envy: "...The sadness at the sight of another's goods and the immoderate desire to acquire them for oneself, even unjustly.

When it wishes grave harm to a neighbor it is a mortal sin: St. Augustine saw envy as "the diabolical sin" (CCC 2539).

The Devil (Deadly Sin 7):

7.   Pride: Undue self-esteem or self-love, which seeks attention and honor and sets oneself in competition with God. Webster's dictionary adds vanity, vainglory, conceit, arrogance, egotism, boastfulness, self-glorification, and selfishness to the definition of pride.

The greatest enemy and obstacle to our freedom is sin. Namely, these seven we just identified and defined. Here is an area where our analogy with the Israelites and Pharaoh falls short. Their original bondage was external; ours is internal. It's a matter of the heart. In fact, it is actually a matter of two hearts:

1.   God's Heart: Sin isn't just breaking a rule, it's breaking a heart. Our Lord sorrowfully revealed his pierced Heart to St. Margaret Mary Alacoque saying, "Behold this Heart which has so loved men, that it has spared nothing, even to exhausting and consuming itself in order to testify to its love. In return, I have received from the greater part only ingratitude, by their irreverence and their sacrilege, and by the coldness and contempt they have for Me in this sacrament of Love." When we sin, we break God's heart.

2.   Your Heart: "The root of all sins lies in a man's heart" (CCC 1873).

Our journey into great freedom is a journey to set your heart free. It's deeply personal; deeply intimate. Tomorrow, we get even more specific in examining our own hearts.

Day 8
An Examination: The Flesh

Yesterday, we established that all sin is close and personal; indeed, it's a matter of the heart. Our enemies aren't just external, but are seeking to attack us at our very core. There is a war and battle that rages within, an inner struggle with the highest of stakes.

Today, we will explore how the "sins of the flesh" affect our hearts, our freedom and our holy desires. A heart that is bound to the flesh unknowingly becomes a slave to *the comforts of this world*. The issue is with man 'in himself'. He sways to what is convenient, comfortable and feels good. The spirit may be willing, but the flesh is weak. In this case, the holy desires which God places in the heart are not taken away altogether, but are left unfulfilled like a star athlete who squanders his talents.

Recall the parable of the Sower and the Seed, considering the seed that fell upon the rocky path, "where they had not much soil, and immediately they sprang up, since they had no depth of soil, but when the sun rose they were scorched; and since they had no root they withered away" (Matthew 13:5-6). Christ himself gives us the interpretation, "...this is he who hears the word and immediately receives it with joy; yet he has no root in himself, but endures for a while, and when tribulation or persecution arises on account of the word, immediately he falls away" (Matthew 13:20-21).

We will be initiating a series of examinations of conscious, beginning with the sins of the flesh. Be honest and authentic; no fronts or masks. Keep in mind that God already knows your heart as well as all the answers.

1. Have I been sexually unfaithful to my spouse (past, current)?

2. Have I visited a topless bar or any place where women are not fully clothed (past, last year, month, week)?

3. Have I viewed pornography or sexually explicit materials (past, last year, month, week)?

4. Have I lusted after another or objectified my spouse (past, current)?

5. Have I flirted with someone other than my spouse (past, current)?

6. Have I used illicit drugs or misused prescription medications (past, last year, month, week)?

7. Have I misused alcohol (past, last year, month, week)?

8. Do I eat an unhealthy diet or fail to get appropriate exercise?

9. Have I raised my voice in anger toward my spouse or children (past, last year, month, week)?

10. Do I frequently argue or disagree with my spouse?

11. Do I lose my temper or get frustrated with people easily?

12. Am I slow to forgive?

Do I have significant problems with sins of the flesh? Do I struggle with lust, wrath, gluttony or sloth? Some of them? All of them? Take a moment to sit quietly and reflect.

Are sins of the flesh your Pharaoh? Is it one or more specifically within this section: lust, wrath, gluttony, or sloth? If you have discovered your Pharaoh, your source of bondage, name it. Renounce it. As a proactive step, plan to get to confession and begin the process of freedom.

Sometimes after we complete an examination of conscious, like Adam, we are tempted to hide in our shame; or like King David, we selfishly seek to hide or cover up our sin. When we're exposed like Adam, who was naked before both God and Eve, we sometimes attempt to hide from others (fig leaves) and even vainly venture to hide from God (see Gen 3:8).

The good news is immediately after Adam sinned (in the very next verse) the Lord was already pursuing, "But the Lord God called to the man, and said to him, "Where are you?" (Gen 3:9). God already knew where Adam was hiding, but in his gentleness, he allowed him to come out of hiding on his own. It's a recurring theme, right? God grants us the freedom to come out or continue to remain in bondage and shame.

The Lord is calling you. He is asking you. He is pursuing you in this very moment:

"Where are you? Where is your heart? I love you. I am close to you even in your sin. You may run and hide from me but I will never run from you. You may be weary of your sinfulness but I will never grow weary. You may be lost but you can be found. You may be blind but I can give you new sight. Your heart may be wounded but I have come to heal and restore. I have already taken your sin and shame and obliterated it. I have come to set your heart free. I have come to give you a new heart. I have come to give you my heart. My light will shine through your wounds. Will you trust me? Will you enter into my heart? Do you love me?"

Day 9
An Examination: The World

Yesterday we began a difficult but necessary process to confront the depravities of our heart. We took a deeper look at sins of the flesh. Today, we take the next step in our three-fold concupiscence: the world.

We aspire to see how the "sins of the world" affect our hearts, our freedom and our holy desires. In a case where a heart is bound to the world, the holy desires that God places in our hearts are choked, suffocated and squeezed out by the world. At best, there is no longer any time for God and the desires of our hearts.

We again recall the parable of the Sower and the Seed, this time relating to the seed that fell upon the thorny path, "and the thorns grew up and choked them" (Matthew 13:7). Christ himself gives us the interpretation, "As for what was sown among thorns, this is he who hears the word, but the cares of the world and the delight in riches choke the word, and it proves unfruitful" (Matthew 13:22).

Let us now enter into our second examination of conscious according to sins of the world. Be honest and authentic. Once again, no fronts or masks. Keep in mind that God already knows your heart as well as all the answers.

1. Do I give the first fruits of my income to the Church and/or charity?

2. Do I spend more money on all forms of entertainment combined than I give to charity?

3. Do I participate in gossip?

4. Do I miss dinner more than 2 nights/week because of work?

5. Do I work on Sunday?

6. Have I stolen anything – including expense report and income taxes (past, recent)?

7. Do my conversations typically revolve around business, sports and news events?

8. Do I attempt to remain constantly up-to-date on news events?

9. Do I spend more time on the media than on my spiritual life?

10. Do I have friendships or business activities that lead me into sin or inappropriate behaviors?

11. Do I envy or experience jealousy regarding the ability, talents, ideas, good-looks, intelligence, clothes, possessions, money, friends, family, of others?

12. Am I saddened or frustrated at the success of others?

13. Do I judge others in my thoughts, words or actions?

14. Do I damage the reputation of others by my words or actions?

15. Do I fail to defend the reputation of others?

Are sins of the world your Pharaoh? Is it just one or both within this section: greed, envy? If you have discovered your Pharaoh, your source of bondage, name it. Renounce it. Plan to get to confession and begin the process of freedom.

We learned yesterday to never hide from the Lord. Jesus Christ, the new Adam, entered fully into our human condition and took on the sins of the world. He carried every sin to the heart of the Father. He bore our suffering, our shame, our guilt, and nailed them to the Cross. He embraced the Cross for our salvation. Clothed with sins of the world, Christ didn't hide from the face of God.

In fact, he did the exact opposite of Adam, "...there was darkness over the whole land...while the sun's light failed...Then Jesus, crying with a loud voice, said, "Father, into thy hands I commit my spirit!" And having said this he breathed his last" (Luke 23:44-46).

If Jesus taught us anything it's that the Father's mercy is infinite, it's limitless. His mercy is unfathomable to the point of scandal. The scandal of the Cross is that Christ died and rose from EVERY sin ever committed in human history. That's right, all of them! Even the absolute darkest characters and most heinous sins ever committed. The grace of the Cross is sufficient; the victory is won. He has already paid the price. We learn what it means to enter into and claim that victory so that we may die and rise to new life with him. And that is exactly what we will set out to do.

We end today as we did yesterday, listening for the Lord calling in our hearts:

"Where are you? Where is your heart? I love you. I am close to you even in your sin. You may run and hide from me but I will never run from you. You may be weary of your sinfulness but I will never grow weary. You may be lost but you can be found. You may be blind but I can give you new sight. Your heart may be wounded but I have come to heal and restore. I have already taken your sin and shame and obliterated it. I have come to set your heart free. I have come to give you a new heart. I have come to give you my heart. My light will shine through your wounds. Will you trust me? Will you enter into my heart? Do you love me?"

Day 10
An Examination: The Devil

"For all that is in the world, the lust of the flesh and the lust of the eyes and *the pride of life*, is not of the Father but is of the world" (1 John 2:16). As the last installment in our threefold concupiscence reflection, we now focus upon the pride of life. The Church has always understood this "pride of life" to relate to the devil who strived to make himself like God. He then offered that very same temptation to Adam and continues to offer it to you and me.

When our hearts are not firmly united to God, the holy desires that God places there are quickly lost. In fact, they are stolen! We read from St. John that the evil one "...comes only to steal and kill and destroy" (John 10:10). The devil craves to consume our desires and send us counterfeit ones in their place. It's God himself who both gives us our holy desires and nourishes them so if we are not united to God, those desires quickly fade.

We see this clearly played out and illustrated in the parable of the Sower and the Seed, this time relating to the seed that fell upon the footpath, "and the birds came and devoured them" (Matthew 13:4). Christ himself gives us the interpretation, "When any one hears the word of the kingdom and does not understand it, the evil one comes and snatches away what is sown in his heart; this is what was sown along the path" (Matthew 13:19).

Today, we enter into our third and final examination of conscious, according to the pride of life. Be honest and authentic. Once again, no fronts or masks. Keep in mind that God already knows your heart as well as all the answers.

1. Do I go to Mass every Sunday?

2. Do I begin and end each day in prayer?

3. Do I have specific times of prayer throughout the day?

4. Do I frequently pause to unite myself to God throughout the day?

5. Do I go to Confession at least once/year?

6. Can I name all of the Ten Commandments?

7. Do I read Scripture on a regular basis?

8. Do I frequently read spiritual books and/or watch spiritual programming?

9. Do I have spiritual conversations with my family and friends on a regular basis?

10. Is my faith involved in every aspect of my life?

11. Do I refuse or resist admitting my weaknesses?

12. Do I rank myself better than others?

13. Am I stubborn or arrogant?

14. Do I assume I am right and others are wrong without ensuring I actually understand them or their ideas?

15. Am I overly concerned about what others think of me?

Is pride your Pharaoh? Do you live your daily life practically on your own, without a true and utter dependence upon God? If you have discovered your Pharaoh, your source of bondage, name it. Renounce it. Plan to get to confession and begin the process of freedom. Looking back over these last three days, if you haven't found anything yet and are still searching for your Pharaoh, go back and take a deeper look. If you still come up empty, then consider yours to be pride.

Pride is the mother of all sin. There exists an element of pride in every sin we commit. We choose what we think is best and turn from the ways of God saying, "My will be done" rather than "Thy will be done." I will make this one easy for all of us; we all have pride. In some cases, it's rather hidden but it's there. As we progress along we will learn how to undo and counteract this destructive pattern.

As in prior days, we conclude our examination of conscience by listening to the gentle and personal calling of our Lord:

"Where are you? Where is your heart? I love you. I am close to you
even in your sin. You may run and hide from me but I will never
run from you. You may be weary of your sinfulness but I will never
grow weary. You may be lost but you can be found. You may be
blind but I can give you new sight. Your heart may be wounded but

I have come to heal and restore. I have already taken your sin and shame and obliterated it. I have come to set your heart free. I have come to give you a new heart. I have come to give you my heart. My light will shine through your wounds. Will you trust me? Will you enter into my heart? I ask you a third time, like my beloved Peter, do you love me?"

Day 11
The Source of Freedom

"But the Lord said to Moses, "Now you shall see what I will do to Pharaoh; for with a strong hand he will send them out, yea, with a strong hand he will drive them out of his land."

"And God said to Moses, "I am the Lord. I appeared to Abraham, to Isaac, and to Jacob, as God Almighty, but by my name the Lord I did not make myself known to them. I also established my covenant with them, to give them the land of Canaan, the land in which they dwelt as sojourners. Moreover, I have heard the groaning of the people of Israel whom the Egyptians hold in bondage and I have remembered my covenant. Say therefore to the people of Israel, 'I am the Lord, and I will bring you out from under the burdens of the Egyptians, and I will deliver you from their bondage, and I will redeem you with an outstretched arm and with great acts of judgment, and I will take you for my people, and I will be your God; and you shall know that I am the Lord your God, who has brought you out from under the burdens of the Egyptians. And I will bring you into the land which I swore to give to Abraham, to Isaac, and to Jacob; I will give it to you for a possession. I am the Lord.'" Moses spoke thus to the people of Israel; but they did not listen to Moses, because of their broken spirit and their cruel bondage. And the Lord said to Moses, "Go in, tell Pharaoh king of Egypt to let the people of Israel go out of his land"
(Exodus 6:1-11).

Do you have any doubts who is fighting for you? We spent three days in the wallows of our sins but alas, God is on our side! As surely as he did for Israel he will do for you. Sent into the world as the "new" Moses, Jesus Christ has the power to break the chains of your bondage and set you free.

If you are still wrestling with this concept of freedom, rest easy as you are in good company. Even Moses missed the mark. He thought it was all about him, struggling to look past his own obstacles and shortcomings. "But Moses said to the Lord, "Behold,

36

the people of Israel have not listened to me; how then shall Pharaoh listen to me, who am a man of uncircumcised lips?" (Exodus 6:12).

The saga intensified as Moses continued to question God, "Behold, I am of uncircumcised lips; how then shall Pharaoh listen to me?" (Exodus 6:30).

Meanwhile, the Lord patiently and assertively affirmed who was in charge:

Exodus - Chapter 7:
- "See, I make you as God to Pharaoh…"
- "You shall speak all that I command you"
- "But I will harden Pharaoh's heart"
- "I multiply my signs and wonders in the land of Egypt"
- "I will lay my hand upon Egypt and bring forth my hosts"
- "And the Egyptians shall know that I am the Lord, when I stretch forth my hand upon Egypt and bring out the people of Israel from among them."
- "I will strike the water that is in the Nile with the rod that is in my hand"

Eventually Moses got it. Seeing God's initiative in action, Moses began to become more and more emboldened with trust. No longer afraid to confront Pharaoh, Moses boldly proclaimed, "Be it as you say, that you may know that there is no one like the Lord our God" (Exodus 8:10). To put it bluntly, Moses was saying, "Whatever Mr. King, Mr. Big Shot, Mr. Pharaoh, say whatever you would like, I'm not scared of you anymore. Even you will come to know that there is no one like our God. The Lord desires to set us free and there is nothing you can say or do about it!"

Moses began to see that God was more powerful than the force currently oppressing his people. He believed it. He harnessed the power of God to set his people free. Yes, God could have done it alone, but he didn't. In typical fashion, he used man to carry his salvific plan, but only after a personal call to act and respond. Moses, Aaron and the Israelites were not passive in this process.

Miracles, signs and wonders followed. An incredible adventure of deliverance took place that was passed down and echoed throughout the ages. With a mighty hand, God delivered them from the hands of the Egyptians. The Lord our God has come to his people and set them free.

For the first time in ages, freedom was at hand for the Israelites. But their journey was not over just yet; in fact, it was just getting started. Something big and vast stood between Egypt and the Promised Land that the people hadn't bargained for.

Day 12
The Inner Conflict

As children of the Almighty, we were created to desire heaven, yet we condemn ourselves and choose against it time and time again. Why do we fall from the resolution to avoid sin? On one hand, we long for what is true, good and fulfilling, yet so often choose counterfeit, destruction and emptiness. Stressed and torn through a sort of spiritual tug-of-war, our journey can seem so frustrating and complicated. Rest assured, we are not alone. Listen to the words of the great evangelist, St. Paul:

"I do not understand my own actions. For I do not do what I want, but I do the very thing I hate...I can will what is right, but I cannot do it. For I do not do the good I want, but the evil I do not want is what I do. Now if I do what I do not want, it is no longer I that do it, but sin which dwells within me" (Romans 7:15-20).

Have you ever felt this way? Do you seem to confess the same sins in the confessional time and time again? So often our Act of Contrition prayer to "firmly resolve, with the help of thy grace, to sin no more and avoid the near occasion of sin" seems so futile. Even St. Paul recognizes the conflict between the good he hungers for and the sin that almost seems to puppeteer his actions.

He continues, "...I see in my members another law at war with the law of my mind and making me captive to the law of sin which dwells in my members. Wretched man that I am! Who will deliver me from this body of death?" (Romans 7: 23-24).

Paul's inner conflict is our inner conflict. It was the external conflict for the Israelites also. Bondage, slavery, captivity and a lack of freedom to do the good that is desired seems to be a universal challenge. Thankfully, St. Paul went to war and battled with this inner struggle and came out on the other side a Saint, victorious over the sin that previously held him captive. As a Jewish scholar versed in the story of the Egyptian bondage, Paul asked the question for our benefit, "Who will deliver me from this body of death?"

By now we should know the answer. The Israelites could not do it alone and neither can we. See Paul's very next line, "Thanks be to God through Jesus Christ our Lord!" (Romans 7:25). It's Jesus, the new Moses, who will deliver us from this body of death. The Lord has already taken the initiative to destroy sin and death once and for all! Building upon the inspired truth in chapter 7, we now look at Romans chapter 8:

"There is therefore now no condemnation for those who are in Christ Jesus. For the law of the Spirit of life in Christ Jesus has set me free from the law of sin and death...sending his own Son in the likeness of sinful flesh and for sin, he condemned sin in the flesh...For those who live according to the flesh set their minds on the things of the flesh, but those who live according to the Spirit set their minds on the things of the Spirit. To set the mind on the flesh is death, but to set the mind on the Spirit is life and peace...But you are not in the flesh, you are in the Spirit, if the Spirit of God really dwells in you...But if Christ is in you, although your bodies are dead because of sin, your spirits are alive because of righteousness. If the Spirit of him who raised Jesus from the dead dwells in you, he who raised Christ Jesus from the dead will give life to your mortal bodies also through his Spirit who dwells in you. So then...if you live according to the flesh you will die, but if by the Spirit you put to death the deeds of the body you will live. For all who are led by the Spirit of God are sons of God. For you did not receive the spirit of slavery to fall back into fear, but you have received the spirit of sonship." (Romans 8:1-16).

The New Testament is a freedom story...and it's infinitely greater than Braveheart (sorry Mel, I mean, uh, William Wallace). In fact, the entire Bible is a freedom story with God himself as the initiator all along. Now I'm going to say something that may be a little shocking to some...God did not send his only Son so that we could *just* get to Heaven. It's not *just* about accepting Jesus and sort of sneaking into Heaven through the merits of the Cross. Certainly, Christ died for us so that we could obtain eternal life, that much can be sure. But God also sent his only Son to set us free! Free from this inner conflict that you, I, Paul and every other human person experiences as a result of sin. And he didn't just die and rise, but sent us his Spirit to dwelt within us. He wants to give us his very life through the Spirit of God dwelling within us. We are children of God and heirs to his inheritance. The Father gives us everything. He gives us his very life. Good news indeed!

Section 4:

Crossing the Wilderness

"...Self-mastery: is a training in human freedom. The alternative is clear: either man governs his passions and finds peace, or he lets himself be dominated by them and becomes unhappy...Self-mastery is a long and exacting work. One can never consider it acquired once and for all. It presupposes renewed effort at all stages of life. The effort required can be more intense in certain periods."

Catechism of the Catholic Church (2339-2342)

Day 13
Crossing the Wilderness

The Israelites were finally free from the hands of the Egyptians. God heard their cries, had compassion upon them, performed mighty miracles and drove them out of their bondage and into a new world. He promised them "a land flowing with milk and honey" (Exodus 3:8) where they could worship him in freedom. But what stood between Egypt and the Promised Land? "He made them wander in the wilderness forty years, until all the generation that had done evil in the sight of the Lord was consumed" (Numbers 32:13).

Even in the Old Testament the evil had to be consumed. It had to be purged before they could enter into the Promised Land. Once again, this Old Testament account has a New Testament spiritual fulfillment that impacts our lives personally and practically today. In St. John's vision of Heaven, he proclaims, "...nothing unclean shall enter it, nor any one who practices abomination or falsehood..." (Revelation 21:27).

Nothing unclean exists in Heaven; everything else will fade. Only love shall pass through the grave into eternal life. This reality should represent our ultimate examination of conscience. Have we reached the state of becoming pure love? If you are anything like me, the easy answer is "no". Therefore, by definition there is a great deal of purging that still needs to take place in our hearts. This is not entirely different than what the Israelites had to overcome, a pathway through purification.

The three states or "ways" of the spiritual life are the Purgative State, the Illuminative State, and the Unitive State. Unfortunately, there is no possible way for us to bypass the first step! During this Purgative state, the soul begins by *actively* working to overcome vices and sins. Later, God himself will father the soul through a more *passive* purgation. We will circle back to active and passive purgation later in our journey.

For souls who are on the pathway to God but have yet to be fully cleansed of imperfections, our hope is that the merciful Father will allow them to continue this process in the next life. This condition is known as purgatory. You see, sin has both temporal and eternal consequences. Jesus' death and resurrection, if we accept it, has saved us from the eternal consequences of sin; a.k.a. hell.

43

Nonetheless, even though we are forgiven and saved from the eternal abyss there are still temporal consequences, consequences in time, that we have to deal with. This purification process begins right now, but if it is not completed on earth, because of God's unfathomable mercy he allows us to finish it even after death. In Purgatory, souls are refined in the fire of God's mercy and love and all that is impure and unclean is burned away. When the soul is completely full of love and love alone, it passes into Heaven.

Purification must take place one way or another. In this life, we are granted the freedom to choose it. In the next, the choice is no longer ours. In one of his famous Wednesday audiences, St. John Paul II proclaimed to the gathered crowd, "We are invited to 'cleanse ourselves from every defilement of body and spirit' (2 Cor 7:1; cf. 1 Jn 3:3), because the encounter with God [Heaven] requires absolute purity. Every trace of attachment to evil must be eliminated, every imperfection of the soul corrected. Purification must be complete, and indeed this is precisely what is meant by the Church's teaching on Purgatory. The term does not indicate a place, but a condition of existence" (General Audience, 4 August 1999).

My friends, our goal is to pass through the Purgative state in this life. This is God's desire for every soul. In modern times, we do health and diet cleanings. Significant money is spent on intensive exercise routines and workout regimens. It's time to experience for ourselves a deeper spiritual workout and cleansing. We said earlier that when you swim in the ocean, you start to smell like fish. The reality is we may stink more than we know, and some significant elbow grease may be required to wash it all away.

The time has come to courageously and willfully enter into the wilderness with Christ. He calls us. He longs to show us a new way and a new life. Undergoing a death and a resurrection, we will be made whole.

> "Therefore, behold, I will allure her, and bring her into the wilderness, and speak tenderly to her" (Hosea 2:14).

The Lord desires to speak to our hearts, gently and directly. In order to be intimate we must leave the world, so to speak, and go away with him. All our cares, worldly distractions and desires must be set aside. He is leading and, in love, we must follow. In the desert, we rediscover our thirst.

In this section, each day we will be given a new spiritual practice. Some are designed specifically for purification, while others are designed more specifically for union with God, which will enkindle love. Without love, we are bankrupt and none of this will amount to anything. "The interior penance of the Christian can be expressed in many and various ways. Scripture and the Fathers insist above all on three forms, fasting, prayer, and almsgiving" (CCC 1434).

- Fasting (mortification) develops depth to overcome weaknesses of the flesh.
- Almsgiving (charity) helps us to overcome the world by rightly ordering the goods of this world.
- Prayer unites us to God and enkindles love, which helps us to withstand the assaults of the devil.

Today, we begin our first spiritual practice. As one of our most precious and limited resources, let us put 'first things first' and give God our time. His tender voice will be our guide as he begins to speak gently to our hearts. His love will carry us through.

Our Pathway through the Wilderness

Enkindle Love:
- **Ten minutes of silence with the Lord each day.**

The Flesh:
1. Lust
2. Gluttony
3. Sloth
4. Wrath

The World:
   5.   Greed
   6.   Envy

The Devil:
   7.   Pride

Day 14
Sanctification of the Soul

Who likes the idea of being purged? Anyone wake up today hoping to find themselves wandering in a wilderness or desert, anxiously awaiting a chance to be pruned and refined in fire? One way or another, it is a necessary step along the path to holiness. You see, God doesn't just desire our salvation, but he desires our sanctification as well.

Let me try to explain. So many Christians focus simply on salvation, whether or not they make it to Heaven. A popular presumption in Christianity is the notion of "once saved always saved." At any given moment in time if you trust in Jesus and accept him as your personal Lord and Savior, you are therefore saved and are rewarded with eternal life. This belief and way of thinking stems from a theological premise that originated from Martin Luther. He believed and proclaimed that man is a "dung heap covered with snow." Essentially, man is corrupted at his core (dung heap), but by the power of the Cross and the grace of God we are made beautiful (covered with snow). God the Father overlooks our depravity and sees the merits of his Son and presto, Heaven is ours. Those who follow this belief generally do not believe in purgatory, this state of deeper "cleansing" to purify us at our very core. This stems from a primary focus on the word 'salvation'. Now don't get me wrong, Catholics also believe in salvation but from a slightly different perspective. As we mentioned yesterday, the salvation won at the Cross saves us from eternal punishment (hell), but we still need to be *cleansed to the core* (all the dung must go away) to enter into Heaven.

Catholic theology takes salvation a step further and places a primary focus on the word sanctification as well. The power of the Cross has an even greater, more efficacious effect as the grace redeemed by Christ is not exhausted though merely a cosmetic covering alone. It doesn't just take something intrinsically ugly and make it *appear* beautiful. It runs much deeper than that. The grace of the Cross is so powerful that it can touch the very depths of us to purify us. This reality is not a one-and-done decision but rather a process. In most cases, it takes an entire lifetime! Thanks be to God that his great love is such that he not only forgives us from our sins but also burns away *all* the consequences of sin. And by the extraordinary, superabundant, unfathomable and limitless mercy of God he grants some souls the opportunity to extend this process even beyond death. Purgatory is a great gift that is directly related to God's mercy and it's directly related to the reality that nothing unclean will enter into Heaven.

Ready for even more good news? During this journey together, we are going to spend forty *days* working to purify our lives. That's much better than forty *years* with Moses in the wilderness, right? We have previously identified the three-headed monster represented in the flesh, the world and the devil. We examined our lives against the seven deadly sins, and even searched within ourselves to name our bondage to sin, our Pharaoh. The next step is to purge, detach and remove the root cause of our problems and replace them with the things of God.

Drawing from the Catechism now, "Self-mastery...is a training in human freedom. The alternative is clear: either man governs his passions and finds peace, or he lets himself be dominated by them and becomes unhappy. Man's dignity therefore requires him to act out of conscious and free choice, as moved and drawn in a personal way from within, and not by blind impulses in himself or by mere external constraint. Man gains such dignity when, ridding himself of all slavery to the passions, he presses forward to his goal by freely choosing what is good and, by his diligence and skill, effectively secures for himself the means suited to this end" (CCC 2339).

Notice the key choice of words used when the Catechism speaks of self-mastery: training in human freedom. That's exactly what we are setting out to do! And although this book is only 40 days of training, "Self-mastery is a long and exacting work. One can never consider it acquired once and for all. It presupposes renewed effort at all stages of life. The effort required can be more intense in certain periods..." (CCC 2342).

Are you ready? Do you need a William Wallace rally cry once again? You have made it this far, so let us call upon the Lord for the courage and strength to press on in our quest for the prize.

Our spiritual practice for today is to begin the purification process by declaring war against the enemies of freedom and charge into battle.

Our Pathway through the Wilderness

Enkindle Love:
- Ten minutes of silence with the Lord each day.

Declaration of War:
- **Declare war against the enemies that seek to enslave us: The Flesh, the World, the Devil.**

The Flesh:
1. Lust
2. Gluttony
3. Sloth
4. Wrath

The World:
5. Greed
6. Envy

The Devil:
7. Pride

Day 15
Grumblings in the Wilderness

The pathway for the Israelites was filled with anxiety, uncertainty and fear of the unknown. Much of their time was spent walking aimlessly in the wilderness, increasingly questioning why they were there and where they were going. We too may experience these same emotions as we wrestle through this seemingly laborious process; but one thing is clear, at the end of the day we have but two choices for our lives:

1. Freedom: "The more one does what is good, the freer one becomes" (CCC 1733).
2. Bondage: Sin creates a proclivity to sin; it engenders vice by repetition of the same acts (CCC 1865).

For the Israelites, this choice wasn't always so clear. For years they begged God to set them free from the bondage of Pharaoh in Egypt, only to respond with resentment and complaints even after a dramatic liberation filled with plagues, miracles and the parting of the Red Sea.

"And all the people of Israel murmured against Moses and Aaron; the whole congregation said to them, "Would that we had died in the land of Egypt! Or would that we had died in this wilderness! Why does the Lord bring us into this land...would it not be better for us to go back to Egypt?" (Numbers 14:2-3).

At first glance these people seem so foolish; but then again, could my story be so different? What do I have to show for the countless ways in which he has saved and protected me throughout my life? The Lord has given me more love, joy, happiness and fulfillment than I could ever have deserved. I've seen and experienced miracles; nonetheless, there are times (more than I'd like to admit) when I've grumbled, murmured and complained. I've pondered if it would be more fun and delightful to return to the source of my bondage versus living in the spirit and love of Christ. The Israelites, as well as each one of us, have moments when we would rather choose to be enslaved and well "fed" than to wander through the hardships of a potentially painful and uncomfortable wilderness. How do you respond when the Lord seeks to purify and prune you, even at times taking something away from you?

For our first active purgation and the remainder of this journey, we seek to control our tongues. We together make a resolution to cease to complain. Let it die. No complaining about work, food, anything your spouse or children do or don't do, being tired, your financial situation, the other drivers on the road, how hot or cold it is, or anything for that matter. "For we all make many mistakes, and if any one makes no mistakes in what he says he is a perfect man, able to bridle the whole body also" (James 3:2).

To counteract our verbal displeasure, let us strive to maintain a spirit of joy and charity in our words, actions and disposition. Smile! Laugh! Give compliments. Praise God for his abundant blessings. Ponder the gifts in your life and be thankful. Bring joy to others!

"From silly devotions and sour-faced saints, good Lord, deliver us!" (St. Teresa of Avila).

Our Pathway through the Wilderness:

Enkindle Love:
- Ten minutes of silence with the Lord each day.
- **Always maintain a spirit of joy and charity.**

Declaration of War:
- Declare war against the enemies that seek to enslave us: The Flesh, the World, the Devil.
- **When at war, there is no complaining.**

The Flesh:
1. Lust
2. Gluttony
3. Sloth
4. Wrath

51

The World:
    5. Greed
    6. Envy

The Devil:
    7. Pride

Day 16

Food for the Journey

"And when the dew had gone up, there was on the face of the wilderness a fine, flake-like thing, fine as hoarfrost on the ground. When the people of Israel saw it, they said to one another, "What is it?" For they did not know what it was. And Moses said to them, "It is the bread which the Lord has given you to eat. This is what the Lord has commanded: 'Gather of it, every man of you, as much as he can eat…" (Exodus 16:14-16).

The Lord always knows what you need. As the Israelites struggled through the wilderness, enduring trials and tribulations in their newfound freedom from Egypt, God was with them. And when they reached the point of utter exhaustion, hungry and desperate for help, he blessed them with the miraculous bread from Heaven to strengthen them along their way:

"And the people of Israel ate the manna forty years, till they came to a habitable land; they ate the manna, till they came to the border of the land of Canaan" (Exodus 16:35).

Just as God sustained his chosen people during their Exodus from Egypt, so too does he nourish us with an even greater spiritual food – the Eucharist. As the ultimate gift and food for the wilderness of our lives, the Eucharist has within it the power to lead us into our Eternal Promised Land! Recall the Eucharistic prayer we pray in Mass each time we participate and receive this sacred bread, "Make holy, therefore, these gifts, we pray, by sending down your Spirit upon them like the dewfall, so that they may become for us the Body and Blood of our Lord Jesus Christ."

The Church has always understood this earthly life to be a pilgrimage and the Eucharist as the spiritual food to lead us along the pathway into the Promised Land. Each of us lives out our own Exodus story, right smack in the middle of salvation history. The Israelites' story becomes our story.

"What material food produces in our bodily life, Holy Communion wonderfully achieves in our spiritual life. Communion with the flesh of the risen Christ...preserves, increases, and renews the life of grace received at Baptism. This growth in Christian life needs the nourishment of Eucharistic Communion, the bread for our pilgrimage until the moment of death..." (CCC 1392).

We all need the Eucharist each and every Sunday; but the reality is, the more the better! Thanks be to God we have the opportunity to receive this spiritual food every day, if we are willing and able. In addition to Sunday, let us aspire to receive the Eucharist at least once per week during daily mass, recalling the words from Exodus, "Every man of you, as much as he can eat."

In addition to the Eucharist, Christ himself speaks specifically of two other spiritual foods:

1) **The Word of God** - "Man shall not live by bread alone, but by every word that proceeds from the mouth of God" (Matthew 4:4). The Word of God is the perfect spiritual food for us because although many can't make it to Mass every day, we can all feed on The Word of God at any time and any place. In the morning, in the middle of the day or night, you can reference your Bible (or your phone/app) easily and conveniently find the readings.

The God of the Universe, the One who is pure spirit, who stands outside of time, infinitely bigger than the biggest thoughts or dreams, has come down from the heavens to speak to us in our human language. His wisdom pierces to the depths of our hearts in ways nothing and no one else can. God awaits us in the Scriptures. Let us find him there daily and allow him to feed us and sustain us.

2) **The Will of God** - "I have food to eat of which you do not know...My food is to do the will of him who sent me, and to accomplish his work" (John 4:32-34).

Our entire journey has been focused upon the will of God and his desire to set us free. We have set out to cooperate with the grace that has been lavished upon us, willing to pay the price to achieve authentic freedom.

These foods are gifts from God, just as surely as the manna was for his chosen people in the days of old. Without that physical food the Israelites would have surely perished in the wilderness. In similar fashion, without our spiritual food from above we will most certainly perish in this world, famished and desperate for the only thing that can bring us ultimate purpose and fulfillment. On the other hand, if we drink deeply of these rich foods, we will transcend this world and already have one foot in the next.

Our Pathway through the Wilderness

Enkindle Love:
- Ten minutes of silence with the Lord each day.
- Always maintain a spirit of joy and charity.
- **Read the Word of God each day.**
- **Attend Mass once per week in addition to Sunday.**

Declaration of War:
- Declare war against the enemies that seek to enslave us: The Flesh, the World, the Devil.
- When at war, there is no complaining.

The Flesh:
1. Lust
2. Gluttony
3. Sloth
4. Wrath

The World:
5. Greed
6. Envy

The Devil:
7. Pride

Day 17
To Conquer Lust

Earlier, we confronted our Pharaoh, naming names and acknowledging that ultimately it is sin that enslaves us. In order to win the war, we had to identify the enemy so that we could build a tactical plan. We have now arrived at the more intense part of the battle, where we go on the offensive against the infamous seven deadly foes.

The first four enemies all fit under sins of the flesh: lust, gluttony, sloth and wrath. In truth, you cannot completely silo any of these; nonetheless, it's beneficial to attack them one-by-one and understand each of them individually. Recall how when we are stuck in habitual sins of the flesh, we live enslaved to the comforts of this world. The issue is with the man "in himself". He sways to what is convenient, comfortable and feels good. As we've heard so many times, the spirit may be willing, but the flesh is weak. It is so easy to become enslaved by our passions and cravings. Thinking back to the rocky soil in Christ's parable, if you have ever had to remove rocks from the soil to plant a new garden, you know that can be real intense work. You have to dig and dig and get really dirty in the process. Ironically enough, I actually did it once while pondering this mystery, and now my flower beds are quite lovely!

Back to our problem, "The harmony in which Adam and Eve had found themselves...is now destroyed: the control of the soul's spiritual faculties over the body is shattered" (CCC 400). Thanks a lot Adam and Eve! Addressing this weakness and lack of harmony, St. Paul proclaimed, "Live by the Spirit, I say, and do not gratify the desires of the flesh. For what the flesh desires is opposed to the Spirit, and what the Spirit desires is opposed to the flesh; for these are opposed to each other, to prevent you from doing what you want" (Galatians 5:16-17).

In a joint effort, we must continue our life of prayer and communion with God to maintain the flow of grace from above, while also diligently working to counteract the effects of sin. For the specific desires of the flesh, one optimal way to regain control and claim your freedom is by mortifying these passions. Adding to our previous examination of conscience:

Am I actively working to make progress against "the flesh"?

- Have I taken tangible steps to safeguard my media access (filters, accountability software, public view space, free access to other family members, etc.)?
- Have I identified the triggers leading me into sin and taken specific actions to avoid them?
- Have I performed penance or mortification by giving up something I like at least once per week?
- Have I performed penance or mortification by doing something I dislike at least once per week?
- Have I performed acts of penance or mortification for my family members?

These are some examples of spiritual practices we must engage in and arm ourselves with if we seek a greater freedom. Let's dive right in and engage combat with our first enemy: Lust.

This form of bondage currently stands at epidemic stages and typically begins enslaving young men (and women) when they are weak, curious and hormonal. Sometimes the decisions and actions made as an adolescent or teenager can immediately and effectively trigger the bondage. Satan doesn't care. Never fighting fair, he exploits our weak spots wherever he can. We have to teach and arm our impressionable youth *before* the devil can get to them.

To tap into the supernatural grace needed and available, we will entrust our purity to the ultimate example, St. Joseph:

> "St. Joseph, help me be pure as you were pure. Help me see the beauty of woman through your eyes. Amen."

Let us recite this prayer daily whenever we encounter temptation. If this is your bondage, you may need to repeat it over and over trusting that the Lord is at your side, fighting to set you free: Believe it! Freedom is possible! Step by step and day by day, this sin will be eradicated and the victory will be yours.

Our Pathway through the Wilderness

Enkindle Love:
- Ten minutes of silence with the Lord each day.
- Always maintain a spirit of joy and charity.
- Read the Word of God each day.
- Attend Mass once per week in addition to Sunday.

Declaration of War:
- Declare war against the enemies that seek to enslave us: The Flesh, the World, the Devil.
- When at war, there is no complaining.

The Flesh:
1. Lust
   - **Pray with St. Joseph every day.**
   - **Break any affair, inappropriate relationship, or flirting.**
   - **Eradicate pornography and/or masturbation.**
   - **Eradicate Rated R movies or shows.**
   - **Eradicate *any* websites that lead to temptation or sin.**
   - **Get accountability software if you cannot do it on your own.**
   - **Take a cold shower once/week. Offer it up for the purity of your spouse, daughter(s) and/or son(s).**

2. Gluttony
3. Sloth
4. Wrath

The World:
5. Greed
6. Envy

The Devil:
7. Pride

Day 18
To Conquer Gluttony

It's timely that we consider gluttony immediately after taking into account lust because they are interrelated in a very powerful way. Food and sex are the two most sensual desires we have in the flesh. God made both of them good as both are needed for survival of the species. To sustain humanity from one generation to the next, we need sex; to sustain each individual person from one day to the next, food is necessary. Consequently, God designed and wired us in such a way that each time we eat or have sex we receive a dumping of dopamine in the brain that essentially says, "Yes, this is good!" The dilemma occurs when this dopamine dependence gets carried away and good and natural desires quickly become uncontrollable cravings for inordinate enjoyment.

In many cases, if one can be disciplined about food (which includes alcohol), then restraint over sexual sins can be accomplished as well. Even back to the Old Testament, the pathway to repentance and transformation has always consisted of prayer, *fasting* and almsgiving. As an essential and incredibly effective way to purify our passions, we gain strength within ourselves when we fast. We grow in our ability to resist temptation, while strengthening habits and virtues more important still.

As some would say in poker, we are going "All in". Once this journey is completed, you are welcome to modify these spiritual practices to fit your preferences, but for these forty days we are taking no stops in our battle to silence the enemies that seek to enslave us. Time to proclaim a fast! For these final three weeks, all alcohol will be eliminated. On Fridays, we will fast on bread and water only (unless you have a health condition that prevents this), even giving up our favorite food.

Remember, Christ himself gave us the spiritual food needed for the journey. To keep the grace flowing, we have begun feeding on the Eucharist, the Word of God and the Will of God. As any physical hunger or desire is experienced during your fast, use this as an opportunity to enter more deeply into the three spiritual foods. Meditate on your deeper hunger and desire for holiness instead, reminding yourself of your intensifying longing for freedom. In the desert, we will rediscover our thirst.

Our Pathway through the Wilderness

Enkindle Love:
- Ten minutes of silence with the Lord each day.
- Always maintain a spirit of joy and charity.
- Read the Word of God each day.
- Attend Mass once per week in addition to Sunday.

Declaration of War:
- Declare war against the enemies that seek to enslave us: The Flesh, the World, the Devil.
- When at war, there is no complaining.

The Flesh:
1. Lust
   - Pray with St. Joseph every day.
   - Break any affair, inappropriate relationship, or flirting.
   - Eradicate pornography and/or masturbation.
   - Eradicate Rated R movies or shows.
   - Eradicate *any* websites that lead to temptation or sin.
   - Get accountability software if you cannot do it on your own.
   - Take a cold shower once/week. Offer it up for the purity of your spouse, daughter(s) and/or son(s).

2. Gluttony
   - **Pray that you will focus more upon Spiritual Food for the journey.**
   - **Fast from alcohol for the remainder of our journey.**
   - **Fast on bread and water each Friday for the remainder of our journey.**
   - **Give up your favorite food for the remainder of our journey.**

3. Sloth
4. Wrath

<u>The World</u>:
5. Greed
6. Envy

<u>The Devil</u>:
7. Pride

Day 19
To Conquer Sloth

I know exactly what you are thinking! When it comes to sloth, we tend to picture an image of a man on his recliner, beer in hand, vegging out on football all day. Or, for the more outdoorsy type, a furry, slow moving creature sitting (or hanging) motionless in a tree. And you are absolutely right, both illustrations represent an element and unique perspective on sloth.

Sloth involves laziness, boredom, lack of passion and idleness. The Pocket Catholic Dictionary defines sloth as "sluggishness of soul or boredom because of the exertion necessary for the performance of a good work. The good work may be a corporal task, such as walking; or a mental exercise, such as writing; or a spiritual duty, such as prayer".

Although our couch-potato man above was accurate, sloth is not just a sin against productivity. More than merely human laziness to avoid hard work, sloth is a sin against God. It's quite possible to be an incredibly hard worker, never to lay on the couch or veg out on sports, news, or TV shows and still commit the sin of sloth.

Sloth is a failure to do your basic duties each and every day. In today's fast-paced, win-at-all-costs world, sloth may be seen more commonly in working too much, just on the wrong things. While some may not be slothful to earn a paycheck, they may be slothful in their devotion to God, their spouse, children, parish community and prayer life.

The devil ventures to attack us if we fall into either of these two pitfalls of sloth. As we have learned, the enemy never sleeps and always has a plan no matter what your orientation or disposition. We have all heard sayings like, "Idle hands are the devil's workshop" or "Idleness is the devil's playground." At the same time, it's also true that, "If the devil can't make you bad he will make you busy." He attacks us from every side, there is seemingly nowhere to hide.

We must come to understand and develop a hierarchy of our daily responsibilities. Your spiritual duty to care for your soul cannot come *if* there happens to be spare time at the end of the day. God desires your first fruits! He wants the best of you, the best of your love. The same bodes true for your family. We often claim we just do not have the time, whether it be dinner as a family, a relaxing and carefree conversation with our spouse or children, or even in the quiet stillness in the presence of God. The question remains: what do we fill our time up with?

Let us pray for the grace from God to open our eyes to see and properly understand our duties within our state of life. Let us pray for the strength to overcome sluggishness and sloth to fulfill those duties. This can begin the very moment you arise each day. A spiritual director once enlightened me that the first thing you need to do is to decide when you will wake up and go to bed every day. When your alarm clock goes off, God is calling you. A day of good works is beckoning you to arise each day and fulfill your calling.

Our Pathway through the Wilderness

Enkindle Love:
- Ten minutes of silence with the Lord each day.
- Always maintain a spirit of joy and charity.
- Read the Word of God each day.
- Attend Mass once per week in addition to Sunday.

Declaration of War:
- Declare war against the enemies that seek to enslave us: The Flesh, the World, the Devil.
- When at war, there is no complaining.

The Flesh:
1. Lust
- Pray with St. Joseph every day.
- Break any affair, inappropriate relationship, or flirting.
- Eradicate pornography and/or masturbation.
- Eradicate Rated R movies or shows.
- Eradicate *any* websites that lead to temptation or sin.

- Get accountability software if you cannot do it on your own.
- Take a cold shower once/week. Offer it up for the purity of your spouse, daughter(s) and/or son(s).

2. Gluttony
   - Pray that you will focus more upon Spiritual Food for the journey.
   - Fast from alcohol for the remainder of our journey.
   - Fast on bread and water each Friday for the remainder of our journey.
   - Give up your favorite food for the remainder of our journey.

3. Sloth
   - **Pray for the grace to properly understand and fulfill your duties within your state of life.**
   - **Set an alarm early enough for morning prayer each day and stick to it. When the alarm chimes, God is calling.**
   - **Set a limit to your media time outside of work.**

4. Wrath

The World:
5. Greed
6. Envy

The Devil:
7. Pride

Day 20

To Conquer Wrath

"Sticks and stones may break my bones but words will never hurt me."

How many times did we hear that line as a child, wondering if it were actually true? Ironically, it's words that tend to hurt us more deeply than anything else. The emotional effects of wrath and anger can be just as devastating, if not more, than any physical harm done.

"You will never amount to anything."
"I don't owe you anything."
"What's wrong with you? What is your problem?"
"You're an idiot."
"I don't care what you think."

All of us have likely been on the receiving end of one of these at some point in our lives. People speak them out of anger in the moment, allowing their anger to get the best of them. Without fully intending it, our anger can seriously wound others. In the case of a parent/child relationship, these wounds can oftentimes last for a lifetime. Unfiltered and unchecked anger can lead to the deadly sin known as wrath, which can be incredibly damaging to other souls as well as our own.

When we examine the times in our lives when we have been angry, a pattern typically arises. It may be certain people, situations or topics that drive us into anger. Discovering what those triggers are can be extremely beneficial so that we stand better prepared the next time they occur. The next time you find yourself getting worked up and upset, pause for a moment, take a deep breath and consider a quick prayer, "Come Holy Spirit. Let my thoughts and words be life-giving and pleasing to you."

Sometimes the people who tend to make us angry are the ones we find it difficult to see God in. Pray for the grace to see in them the Hidden Face of Christ. Imagine the amount of internal suffering they must be going through, the suffering Christ inside of them. As Plato once said, "Be kind, for everyone you meet is fighting a hard battle."

As Christians, we are to bring Christ with us into this broken world. St. Mother Teresa used to say, "Charity kills conflict." Let's start with those closest to us to build up our spiritual muscles – our family, our friends and our co-workers. Don't let a day go by without speaking words of life-giving love into their day. Build them up rather than tearing them down. Find the good in them; find God in them. And let them know that you have noticed it.

Our Pathway through the Wilderness

Enkindle Love:
- Ten minutes of silence with the Lord each day.
- Always maintain a spirit of joy and charity.
- Read the Word of God each day.
- Attend Mass once per week in addition to Sunday.

Declaration of War:
- Declare war against the enemies that seek to enslave us: The Flesh, the World, the Devil.
- When at war, there is no complaining.

The Flesh:
1. Lust
- Pray with St. Joseph every day.
- Break any affair, inappropriate relationship, or flirting.
- Eradicate pornography and/or masturbation.
- Eradicate Rated R movies or shows.
- Eradicate *any* websites that lead to temptation or sin.
- Get accountability software if you cannot do it on your own.
- Take a cold shower once/week. Offer it up for the purity of your spouse, daughter(s) and/or son(s).

2. Gluttony
   - Pray that you will focus more upon Spiritual Food for the journey.
   - Fast from alcohol for the remainder of our journey.
   - Fast on bread and water each Friday for the remainder of our journey.
   - Give up your favorite food for the remainder of our journey.

3. Sloth
   - Pray for the grace to properly understand and fulfill your duties within your state of life.
   - Set an alarm early enough for morning prayer each day and stick to it. When the alarm chimes, God is calling.
   - Set a limit to your media time outside of work.

4. Wrath
   - **Pray for the grace to see the Hidden Face of Christ in those who you tend to get angry with. Pray for them and forgive them.**
   - **Give a heartfelt compliment to your spouse and children every day.**
   - **Give a heartfelt compliment to your boss, co-workers and employees every day.**

The World:
5. Greed
6. Envy

The Devil:
7. Pride

Day 21
To Conquer Greed

The next two enemies both fit under sins of the world: greed and envy. When our hearts are bound to the world the holy desires that God places within us are choked, suffocated and squeezed out. At best, there is no longer any time for God and the desires of our hearts.

During this part of our journey, we must continue our life of prayer and communion with God while maintaining deliberate diligence to counteract the effects of sin. The last four days were spent examining the flesh, attempting to mortify our passions and liberate our bondage. Now we turn to the sins of the world:

Am I actively working to make progress against "the world"?

- Have I actively avoided activities to spend more time on my spiritual life?
- Do I have a specific time limit on media consumption to "free up" time that I can spend with God, family and friends?
- Have I ever changed the nature of a friendship or business relationship that leads to sin?
- Do I have a budget that I follow with the appropriate person?
- Do I forgo material desires so that I can be more charitable to the Church and other people? Do I live below my means?

These are some examples of spiritual practices that we can engage in to arm ourselves as we seek a greater freedom from the grips and suffocation of the world. Christ proclaimed, "I have said this to you, that in me you may have peace. In the world you have tribulation; but be of good cheer, I have overcome the world" (John 16:33).

Let's charge right in and engage combat with our first enemy: greed.

"Put to death therefore what is earthly in you: fornication, impurity, passion, evil desire, and covetousness, which is idolatry" (Colossians 3:5). Scripture equates covetousness, which is another word for greed, with idolatry. In fact, anything we place above God in our hearts and minds can become an idol, even if it can be construed as a good thing. As such, Scripture places a bone-chilling emphasis on money as highlighted in the following verses:

- The eye of the covetous man is insatiable in his portion of iniquity: he will not be satisfied till he consumes his own soul (Sirach 14:9).
- The love of money is the root of all evil (1 Tim 6:10).
- No one can serve two masters; for either he will hate the one and love the other, or he will be devoted to the one and despise the other. You cannot serve God and mammon (Matthew 6:24).

I've heard it said that you can have money, you just cannot let money have you. Pray for the grace to see money as God's money, a tool properly used to bless others. It's not for you to possess or indeed it will possess you. "The precept of detachment from riches is obligatory for entrance into the Kingdom of Heaven" (CCC 2544).

St. Luke gives us the antidote, "...give alms; provide yourselves with purses that do not grow old, with a treasure in the heavens that does not fail, where no thief approaches and no moth destroys. For where your treasure is, there will your heart be also." (Luke 12: 33–34)

Once again, it's a matter of the heart, and God desires to set your heart free.

Our Pathway through the Wilderness

Enkindle Love:
- Ten minutes of silence with the Lord each day.
- Always maintain a spirit of joy and charity.
- Read the Word of God each day.
- Attend Mass once per week in addition to Sunday.

Declaration of War:
- Declare war against the enemies that seek to enslave us: The Flesh, the World, the Devil.
- When at war, there is no complaining.

The Flesh:
1. Lust
   - Pray with St. Joseph every day.
   - Break any affair, inappropriate relationship, or flirting.
   - Eradicate pornography and/or masturbation.
   - Eradicate Rated R movies or shows.
   - Eradicate *any* websites that lead to temptation or sin.
   - Get accountability software if you cannot do it on your own.
   - Take a cold shower once/week. Offer it up for the purity of your spouse, daughter(s) and/or son(s).

2. Gluttony
   - Pray that you will focus more upon Spiritual Food for the journey.
   - Fast from alcohol for the remainder of our journey.
   - Fast on bread and water each Friday for the remainder of our journey.
   - Give up your favorite food for the remainder of our journey.

3. Sloth
    - Pray for the grace to properly understand and fulfill your duties within your state of life.
    - Set an alarm early enough for morning prayer each day and stick to it. When the alarm chimes, God is calling.
    - Set a limit to your media time outside of work.

4. Wrath
    - Pray for the grace to see the Hidden Face of Christ in those who you tend to get angry with. Pray for them and forgive them.
    - Give a heartfelt compliment to your spouse and children every day.
    - Give a heartfelt compliment to your boss, co-workers and employees every day.

The World:
5. Greed
    - **Pray for the grace to see money as God's money, a tool properly used to bless others.**
    - **Almsgiving: Graciously and generously use your money for God and others. Discover your favorite charities and bless them with your gifts.**
    - **Live below your means. Cut back on personal expenses of entertainment and luxury.**
    - **Eat dinner together with your family at least 5 nights a week.**

6. Envy

The Devil:
7. Pride

Day 22
To Conquer Envy

St. Augustine identified envy as "the diabolical sin". We know that all sin comes forth from the evil one so why does St. Augustine make such a unique distinction for this vice?

Like many common iniquities, envy usually finds its beginnings in a more subtle form: jealousy. For example, if you're neighbor has a really nice car or refreshing swimming pool and it drives you to wish you had one, that is jealousy. Seemingly harmless as first, unchecked jealousy can quickly take it to the next level and really start to do damage. Not only do you want what others have and maybe even seek to acquire it unjustly, but you wish they didn't have it at all and would even desire for harm to fall upon them in order that it be taken away all together. Even if you cannot have what they have, you would be happy if something bad happened to their gift or possession, as in their new car gets scratched, or worse yet, involved in a car accident. A diabolical, wicked sin indeed!

"God created man for incorruption, and made him in the image of his own eternity, but through the devil's envy death entered the world, and those who belong to his party experience it" (Wisdom 2:23-24).

Satan exists eternally envious of humanity! God created mankind in his image and likeness and made us for everlasting life. Mere mortals we are, whom the angels (even fallen angels) tower above in intellect. So why such envy? Some have questioned whether it was specifically the communion of persons, this deep union between man and woman in which we reflect God's Trinitarian image that Satan was envious of.

"God in his deepest mystery is not a solitude, but a family, since he has in himself fatherhood, sonship, and the essence of a family, which is love" (St. John Paul II). He bestows on us the dignity to participate in this deepest of mysteries, the communion of life-giving love. From the very beginning, this was granted to Adam and Eve; but in his insatiable envy, Satan literally could not stand it. Longing to take away this gift at all costs, he will kill, steal and destroy to eliminate our inheritance. Rejoicing (if you can call it that) when we suffer and our harmonious union is shattered.

Sobered by this newfound understanding of the spiritual warfare at hand, let us honestly look within ourselves and assess this particular imperfection once again:

- Do I envy or experience jealousy regarding the ability, talents, ideas, good-looks, intelligence, clothes, possessions, money, friends, family, of others?
- Am I saddened or frustrated at the success of others?
- Do I judge others in my thoughts, words or actions?
- Do I damage the reputation of others by my words or actions?
- Do I fail to defend the reputation of others?

"Love is patient and kind; love is not jealous..." (1 Cor 13:4). Thankfully the sins of the world (greed and envy) can be overcome through the virtue affectionately known as charity. Charity, in efficacious and convincing fashion, conquers any roots of envy in our hearts. "Envy represents a form of sadness and therefore a refusal of charity..."(CCC 2540).

Jesus calls us to a much deeper standard than by simply not being envious towards one another, "A new commandment I give to you, that you love one another; even as I have loved you, that you also love one another. By this all men will know that you are my disciples, if you have love for one another" (John 13:34-35).

As disciples of Christ, we have no room for jealousy or envy in our hearts. Leading to bitterness, resentment, depression and distress, it aims to isolate and enslave us. To love more fully is to enter into greater freedom.

Our Pathway through the Wilderness

Enkindle Love:
- Ten minutes of silence with the Lord each day.
- Always maintain a spirit of joy and charity.
- Read the Word of God each day.
- Attend Mass once per week in addition to Sunday.

Declaration of War:
- Declare war against the enemies that seek to enslave us: The Flesh, the World, the Devil.
- When at war, there is no complaining.

The Flesh:
1. Lust
   - Pray with St. Joseph every day.
   - Break any affair, inappropriate relationship, or flirting.
   - Eradicate pornography and/or masturbation.
   - Eradicate Rated R movies or shows.
   - Eradicate *any* websites that lead to temptation or sin.
   - Get accountability software if you cannot do it on your own.
   - Take a cold shower once/week. Offer it up for the purity of your spouse, daughter(s) and/or son(s).

2. Gluttony
   - Pray that you will focus more upon Spiritual Food for the journey.
   - Fast from alcohol for the remainder of our journey.
   - Fast on bread and water each Friday for the remainder of our journey.
   - Give up your favorite food for the remainder of our journey.

3. Sloth
   - Pray for the grace to properly understand and fulfill your duties within your state of life.
   - Set an alarm early enough for morning prayer each day and stick to it. When the alarm chimes, God is calling.
   - Set a limit to your media time outside of work.

4. Wrath
- Pray for the grace to see the Hidden Face of Christ in those who you tend to get angry with. Pray for them and forgive them.
- Give a heartfelt compliment to your spouse and children every day.
- Give a heartfelt compliment to your boss, co-workers and employees every day.

The World:
5. Greed
- Pray for the grace to see money as God's money, a tool properly used to bless others.
- Almsgiving: Graciously and generously use your money for God and others. Discover your favorite charities and bless them with your gifts.
- Live below your means. Cut back on personal expenses of entertainment and luxury.
- Eat dinner together with your family at least 5 nights a week.

6. Envy
- **Pray for the grace to love your neighbors as Christ loves you and wish nothing but the best for them.**
- **Offer praise and thanksgiving to God every day for the gifts you have received.**
- **Celebrate the success of others and stop viewing life as a competition.**

The Devil:
7. Pride

Day 23
To Conquer Pride

My friends, we have reached the last of the seven deadly sins, but it could be argued that we should have covered this one first because pride can be found at the root of every sin we commit. In essence, in each of our offenses we choose our way versus God's way, our will rather than his will. Yes, pride stretches into all categories of concupiscence: the flesh, the world and perhaps most fittingly, the devil.

St. John tells us that the evil one "...comes only to steal and kill and destroy" (John 10:10). When we are not united in communion with God, the holy desires that God places in our hearts are entirely taken. The devil plots to steal our desires and send us counterfeits in their place. It's God himself who both gives us our holy desires and nourishes them, so when our divine union dissipates, the holy desires quickly fade. This referred to the seed that fell upon the footpath, "and the birds came and devoured them" (Matthew 13:4).

At the very core of Satan's fall was pride. Let us take a moment to consider his infamous descent from grace. God created angels utterly beautiful. They exist as servants and messengers with a superior intellect compared to that of a mere human. The name Lucifer itself means light-bearer. Nevertheless, God granted the angels the same incredible gift that he granted us: freedom. Just like us they are free to choose, but due to their superior intellects the choices they make are final. Satan was created in freedom and for freedom, yet this is precisely the gift he is perpetually trying to steal from us now. He seeks to steal our freedom, steal what is deepest in our hearts and bind us in the chains of slavery. These are the chains of his own self-inflicted misery.

It has been said that hell wasn't created to punish us, but that it exists simply as a radical expression of the gift of freedom that God has bestowed upon us. God means it when he definitively declares those first three words to humanity, "You are free...", allowing mankind to choose even so much as eternal separation from himself. As we've seen, he relentlessly works to win us back through sacrificial love, but ultimately the choice is ours.

"There are only two kinds of people in the end: those who say to God, "Thy will be done," and those to whom God says, in the end, "Thy will be done" (C.S. Lewis). What a powerful force of freedom we have been given!

Scripture scholars have attributed the following statements in the Bible to the fall of Lucifer:

- "Because your heart is proud, and you have said, 'I am a god…'" (Ezekiel 28:1).
- "How you are fallen from heaven [because]…You said in your heart,
  - 'I will ascend to heaven; above the stars of God
  - I will set my throne on high;
  - I will sit on the mount of assembly in the far north;
  - I will ascend above the heights of the clouds,
  - I will make myself like the Most High" (Isaiah 14:12-14).
  - "I will not serve" (Jeremiah 2:20).

Consider these the "I will" statements of the devil. Pride runs deep in the heart of the evil one and notice the exactness in the way in which he tempted humanity from the beginning, "But the serpent said to the woman, "You will not die…when you eat of it your eyes will be opened, and you will be like God, knowing good and evil" (Genesis 3:4-5).

Adam and Eve found themselves conversing with the subtle serpent rather than enjoying their divine union with the Lord and one another. That was their first mistake. Conversing with a fallen angel with a superior intellect, without talking with God; well, he will trick you every single time.

To withstand the temptations of the devil, we must recommit to uniting ourselves to God more fully through prayer. A choice not to pray is a critically clear sign of pride illuminating a belief that we can live life on our own without the need for God. If we fail to cultivate a daily prayer life, "Thy" will inevitably starts becoming "My" will.

Am I actively working to make progress against "the devil"?

77

- Do I begin and end each day with prayer?
- Do I complete an examination of conscience every night?
- Do I find time for silence with God every day?
- Do I go to Confession at least once per month? Once per year?
- Do I have a spiritual plan for my life?

Simply stated, we conquer the devil through prayer. Look below at 'Our Pathway through the Wilderness'. Although pride was covered last, we have been strategically including prayer in each of the other six areas. This was intentional because an element of pride involves itself in every area of sin.

Our Pathway through the Wilderness

Enkindle Love:
- Ten minutes of silence with the Lord each day.
- Always maintain a spirit of joy and charity.
- Read the Word of God each day.
- Attend Mass once per week in addition to Sunday.

Declaration of War:
- Declare war against the enemies that seek to enslave us: The Flesh, the World, the Devil.
- When at war, there is no complaining.

The Flesh:
1. Lust
   - Pray with St. Joseph every day.
   - Break any affair, inappropriate relationship, or flirting.
   - Eradicate pornography and/or masturbation.
   - Eradicate Rated R movies or shows.
   - Eradicate *any* websites that lead to temptation or sin.

- Get accountability software if you cannot do it on your own.
- Take a cold shower once/week. Offer it up for the purity of your spouse, daughter(s) and/or son(s).

2. Gluttony
   - Pray that you will focus more upon Spiritual Food for the journey.
   - Fast from alcohol for the remainder of our journey.
   - Fast on bread and water each Friday for the remainder of our journey.
   - Give up your favorite food for the remainder of our journey.

3. Sloth
   - Pray for the grace to properly understand and fulfill your duties within your state of life.
   - Set an alarm early enough for morning prayer each day and stick to it. When the alarm chimes, God is calling.
   - Set a limit to your media time outside of work.

4. Wrath
   - Pray for the grace to see the Hidden Face of Christ in those who you tend to get angry with. Pray for them and forgive them.
   - Give a heartfelt compliment to your spouse and children every day.
   - Give a heartfelt compliment to your boss, co-workers and employees every day.

The World:
5. Greed
   - Pray for the grace to see money as God's money, a tool properly used to bless others.

- Almsgiving: Graciously and generously use your money for God and others. Discover your favorite charities and bless them with your gifts.
- Live below your means. Cut back on personal expenses of entertainment and luxury.
- Eat dinner together with your family at least 5 nights a week.

6. Envy
   - Pray for the grace to love your neighbors as Christ loves you and wish nothing but the best for them.
   - Offer praise and thanksgiving to God every day for the gifts you have received.
   - Celebrate the success of others and stop viewing life as a competition.

The Devil:
7. Pride
   - **Recommit to the prayers we have begun above because pride abides at the root of every sin.**

Day 24
More Pride to Conquer

Moses, the one who led the Israelites from captivity into freedom, received the Ten Commandments from God on Mount Sinai. In the *new* Exodus story, Jesus "...went up on the mountain, and when he sat down his disciples came to him. And he opened his mouth and taught them, saying: "Blessed are the poor in spirit, for theirs is the kingdom of heaven" (Matthew 5:1-3).

Attacking quite possibly the deepest and most staunch enemy of freedom, Jesus initiated the Beatitudes by equipping us with pride's most feared adversary: humility. It is hard, if not impossible, to truly possess any other virtue if we lack in humility. Simply put, the opposite of humility is pride. Within every sin committed, there is an element of pride at its core. In the words of St. Augustine, "It was pride that changed angels into devils; it is humility that makes men as angels." If our other virtues are filled with pride, then they lack the authenticity to be classified as virtues at all. "Humility is the root, mother, nurse, foundation, and bond of all virtue," St. John Chrysostom once remarked.

If there is a sin in your life that you just cannot seem to shake, and if you've tried countless times through you own efforts and prayers but continue to bring it back to the confessional time and time again, then it's quite possible that the underlying issue is pride, with humility as the hidden solution. Sometimes progress is unable to be made until our pride is shattered and we are broken. The Lord desires a meek and humble heart, one that approaches him transparently, intimately, authentically and humbly. What good would it accomplish to free us from one sin if we were to go about it boosting of *our* heroic efforts, the strength of *our* will, while continuing to judge others? We essentially trade in one sin only to take on several others, all while failing to recognize the greater sin (pride) than the one we are working so hard to cleanse. Sometimes it is pride itself that the Lord wishes to purge; while therefore, in his infinite wisdom, allowing us to struggle in the other sin. The Lord desires men and women of great humility. When he finds a soul with a humble heart, there is no limit to what he can do, no restriction to what he can accomplish and no sin that he cannot obliterate in his mercy!

Consider the humility within the Holy Family:

Jesus:

"Christ Jesus, who, though he was in the form of God, did not count equality with God a thing to be grasped, but emptied himself, taking the form of a servant, being born in the likeness of men. And being found in human form he humbled himself and became obedient unto death, even death on a cross." Therefore God has highly exalted him and bestowed on him the name which is above every name, that at the name of Jesus every knee should bow, in heaven and on earth and under the earth, and every tongue confess that Jesus Christ is Lord, to the glory of God the Father" (Philippians 2:5-11).

Mary:

"And Mary said, "My soul magnifies the Lord, and my spirit rejoices in God my Savior, for he has regarded the low estate of his handmaiden. For behold, henceforth all generations will call me blessed...he has scattered the proud in the imagination of their hearts, he has put down the mighty from their thrones, and exalted those of low degree; he has filled the hungry with good things, and the rich he has sent empty away" (Luke 1: 46-53).

St. Louis de Montfort testified that the devil flees from Mary precisely because of her humility. In his pride, he simply cannot stand it to get crushed (see Genesis 3:15) by a mere human. "The...devil is even more humbled to see himself under the feet of the Blessed Virgin Mary, the most humble person who has ever been, than to feel crushed by the arms of the Almighty" (True Devotion).

Joseph:

Unlike Mary, we cannot quote St. Joseph because not a word of his was spoken in all of Scripture. St. Joseph remained content to be hidden as his foundation was centered around God, not himself. Bearing no desire to be in the limelight or draw attention to himself,

82

his example teaches us an incredibly valuable and absolutely essential element in the spiritual life...It's not about YOU!

By bringing Jesus, Mary and Joseph into your spiritual life, the pride in your heart will begin to be melted away and replaced with humility. Paradoxically, the smaller you become the greater your strength over the devil will be. His tricks and empty promises will no longer have dominion over your life and seize you in bondage. Mother Teresa aspired to be small enough to fit into the heart of Christ. Resting there, we are hidden from the trappings of the evil one. Be humble, become smaller and smaller and be set free!

Let us pray the following "Litany of Humility" each day hereafter:

Litany of Humility:
O Jesus! meek and humble of heart, Hear me.
From the desire of being esteemed, Deliver me, Jesus.
From the desire of being loved, Deliver me, Jesus.
From the desire of being extolled, Deliver me, Jesus.
From the desire of being honored, Deliver me, Jesus.
From the desire of being praised, Deliver me, Jesus.
From the desire of being preferred to others, Deliver me, Jesus.
From the desire of being consulted, Deliver me, Jesus.
From the desire of being approved, Deliver me, Jesus.
From the fear of being humiliated, Deliver me, Jesus.
From the fear of being despised, Deliver me, Jesus.
From the fear of suffering rebukes, Deliver me, Jesus.
From the fear of being calumniated, Deliver me, Jesus.
From the fear of being forgotten, Deliver me, Jesus.
From the fear of being ridiculed, Deliver me, Jesus.
From the fear of being wronged, Deliver me, Jesus.
From the fear of being suspected, Deliver me, Jesus.
That others may be loved more than I,
Jesus, grant me the grace to desire it.
That others may be esteemed more than I, Jesus, grant me the grace to desire it.
That, in the opinion of the world, Jesus, grant me the grace to desire it.
others may increase and I may decrease, Jesus, grant me the grace to desire it.

That others may be chosen and I set aside, Jesus, grant me the grace to desire it.

That others may be praised and I unnoticed, Jesus, grant me the grace to desire it.

That others may be preferred to me in everything, Jesus, grant me the grace to desire it.

That others may become holier than I, provided that I may become as holy as I should, Jesus, grant me the grace to desire it.

Amen.

Congratulations! We have just completed our blueprint of active spiritual exercises to guide us through the wilderness. Keep the following two pages bookmarked in a way that you can always quickly and easily return to them. This is not meant to be an exhaustive, comprehensive list, so feel free to customize and personalize throughout the different stages of your life. You can always come back and rework this process anew.

Our Pathway through the Wilderness

Enkindle Love:
- Ten minutes of silence with the Lord each day.
- Always maintain a spirit of joy and charity.
- Read the Word of God each day.
- Attend Mass once per week in addition to Sunday.

Declaration of War:
- Declare war against the enemies that seek to enslave us: The Flesh, the World, the Devil.
- When at war, there is no complaining.

The Flesh:
1. Lust
   - Pray with St. Joseph every day.
   - Break any affair, inappropriate relationship, or flirting.
   - Eradicate pornography and/or masturbation.
   - Eradicate Rated R movies or shows.
   - Eradicate *any* websites that lead to temptation or sin.
   - Get accountability software if you cannot do it on your own.
   - Take a cold shower once/week. Offer it up for the purity of your spouse, daughter(s) and/or son(s).

2. Gluttony
   - Pray that you will focus more upon Spiritual Food for the journey.
   - Fast from alcohol for the remainder of our journey.
   - Fast on bread and water each Friday for the remainder of our journey.
   - Give up your favorite food for the remainder of our journey.

3. Sloth
   - Pray for the grace to properly understand and fulfill your duties within your state of life.
   - Set an alarm early enough for morning prayer each day and stick to it. When the alarm chimes, God is calling.
   - Set a limit to your media time outside of work.

4. Wrath
   - Pray for the grace to see the Hidden Face of Christ in those who you tend to get angry with. Pray for them and forgive them.
   - Give a heartfelt compliment to your spouse and children every day.
   - Give a heartfelt compliment to your boss, co-workers and employees every day.

The World:

5. Greed

- Pray for the grace to see money as God's money, a tool properly used to bless others.
- Almsgiving: Graciously and generously use your money for God and others. Discover your favorite charities and bless them with your gifts.
- Live below your means. Cut back on personal expenses of entertainment and luxury.
- Eat dinner together with your family at least 5 nights a week.

6. Envy

- Pray for the grace to love your neighbors as Christ loves you and wish nothing but the best for them.
- Offer praise and thanksgiving to God every day for the gifts you have received.
- Celebrate the success of others and stop viewing life as a competition.

The Devil:

7. Pride

- Recommit to the prayers we have begun above because pride abides at the root of every sin.
- Bring the entire Holy Family into your spiritual life and ask them to teach you humility.
- Pray the Litany of Humility each day for the remainder of our journey.

Day 25
Deliver Me, Lord!

We have spent the vast majority of our time in the wilderness dealing with the primary sources of our bondage, namely, the seven deadly sins. And rightfully so! Scripture is filled with references that ensure us the freedom that God longs to restore us to is a freedom from the bondage of sin.

Before Christ was even born an angel appeared to Joseph and proclaimed, "Joseph, son of David, do not fear to take Mary your wife, for that which is conceived in her is of the Holy Spirit; she will bear a son, and you shall call his name Jesus, for he will save his people from their sins." (Matthew 1:20-21). St. Paul later affirmed, "For freedom Christ has set us free..." (Galatians 5:1). Finally, Christ himself undeniably declared, "Truly, truly, I say to you, every one who commits sin is a slave to sin" (John 8:34).

We have engaged our enemy directly in this battle over sin, relying upon a renewed relationship with Christ, a recommitted daily prayer life and God's superabundant grace. A new foundation has been laid, one built on virtues, that will help us to not only avoid and counteract the effects of sin, but also empower us to overcome the proclivity towards these sins. It's a battle between gravity and grace, the flesh and the spirit. Half of the battle is simply in knowing that you are in one with a defined plan of attack already in place. Thanks be to God for the progress we have made thus far!

That being said, there exists outside sources of bondage as well. Sometimes there can be things well below the surface that have caused us intense pain or inflicted deep-seeded wounds. The pain is so gripping that many of our sins or addictions become a manifestation of our attempts to cope. We try to escape reality for a moment to ease the pain, numb the senses and release the tension, even periodically choosing a counterfeit good that offers us momentary satisfaction rather than having to stare reality in the face and struggle through the process of healing and freedom. Like the Israelites in the wilderness, we habitually choose our known bondage rather than walk the journey to freedom. A deeper cycle of sin may ultimately develop which ends up causing even stronger chains of bondage and more painful, penetrating wounds. Quite disconcerting, to say the least.

So, what are these sources of bondage? As countless and unfortunate realities of a fallen world, they were typically caused by sin (ours or someone else's) and in turn, have the power to cause us to give into sin. Let's name just a few, and as they are named see if any strike you personally. Notice if any of these causes you to cringe. I encourage you to offer a quick prayer before you work through this list. God may desire to reveal something you are unaware of.

"Come Holy Spirit, the Sanctifier! Shine light on the deepest and darkest areas in my life. Bring into light that which is hidden so that it may be burned away in the fire of your love. Amen."

Take a moment and read the following list slowly, pausing between each one:

Spirits of Bondage:
- Spirit of Fear
- Spirit of Rejection
- Spirit of Failure
- Spirit of Sadness
- Spirit of Loneliness
- Spirit of a Poor Self-Image
- Spirit of Fatherlessness (An Orphan Spirit)
- Spirit of Never Feeling Loved or Unworthy of Love
- Spirit of Shame
- Spirit of Guilt
- Spirit of Apathy
- Spirit of Distrust
- Spirit of Doubt
- Spirit of Skepticism
- Spirit of Regret
- Spirit of Weakness
- Spirit of Uselessness
- Spirit of Never Measuring Up
- Spirit of Hopelessness

Do you personally identify with any of these? Oftentimes something from our past has precipitated one of these deep wounds – a broken family, a parent leaving, physical or emotional abuse, sexual sin, and so on. In his infinite goodness and mercy, the Lord longs to shine his light through your deepest wounds and deliver you. The Divine Physician has come to heal the sick and broken-hearted.

For additional reading and an even deeper dive into deliverance from these or other spirits of bondage, check out "Unbound: A Practical Guide to Deliverance from Evil Spirits" by Neal Lazano.

For today, I would simply like for us to speak with the power and authority of Christ over each spirit of bondage we've considered. Again, be attentive to the revealing power of the Holy Spirit as you pray:

In the name of Jesus, I renounce the spirit of fear.
In the name of Jesus, I renounce the spirit of rejection.
In the name of Jesus, I renounce the spirit of failure.
In the name of Jesus, I renounce the spirit of sadness.
In the name of Jesus, I renounce the spirit of loneliness.
In the name of Jesus, I renounce the spirit of a poor self-image.
In the name of Jesus, I renounce the spirit of fatherlessness.
In the name of Jesus, I renounce the spirit of never feeling loved or unworthy of love.
In the name of Jesus, I renounce the spirit of shame.
In the name of Jesus, I renounce the spirit of guilt.
In the name of Jesus, I renounce the spirit of apathy.
In the name of Jesus, I renounce the spirit of distrust.
In the name of Jesus, I renounce the spirit of doubt.
In the name of Jesus, I renounce the spirit of skepticism.
In the name of Jesus, I renounce the spirit of regret.
In the name of Jesus, I renounce the spirit of weakness.
In the name of Jesus, I renounce the spirit of uselessness.
In the name of Jesus, I renounce the spirit of never measuring up.
In the name of Jesus, I renounce the spirit of hopelessness.

In the name of Jesus, I renounce any and all evil spirits. Rather, I choose the Spirit of God to surround me, protect me, sanctify me, heal me, cast out my sins, remember them no more and blot them out. I choose the Spirit of God to animate me, illuminate me, burn away any doubt, fear or distraction, bring me joy, help me trust, increase my faith, restore my hope, and to fill and overwhelm me with divine love.

In the name of Jesus, I claim his victory as mine! I claim his Father as mine! I claim his freedom over the wickedness and snares of the devil! In the name of Jesus, I claim freedom. Amen!

Be humble but be bold; Christ has won the victory. We cannot boast on our own but can boast of the power of the Crucified and Risen One. It's up to us to believe it, claim it and take back what is rightfully ours. The power of his infinite love destroyed death itself once and for all. Love has conquered the grave, an eternal, everlasting triumph over death!

Day 26
What is Truth?

"Pilate said to Jesus, "What is truth?" (John 18:38).

In the so called postmodern world that we currently find ourselves in, this question is haunting. The contention of objective vs. subjective truth might be one the greatest issues that plagues our society, as it continues to distort and deform the hearts and minds of countless souls, especially our youth. This might sound crazy but at least Pilate asked the question! Popular culture has evidently become so intellectually 'wise' that we have now grown up to believe that we are beyond even asking this question. As a society, we no longer seek objective truth; rather, it has become relative to each individual. To make matters worse, if the beliefs and actions of individuals are challenged, then that person immediately becomes labeled as old-fashioned, non tolerant and an uncompassionate bigot. Truly we live in a "dictatorship of relativism" as Pope Benedict XVI pointed out.

The problem is truth and freedom are profoundly interrelated. Deeply concerned and determined to restore our freedom Christ explained, "If you continue in my word, you are truly my disciples, and you will know the truth, and the truth will make you free" (John 8:31-32).

Like many modern Americans, the Jews just simply failed to understand. "We are descendants of Abraham, and have never been in bondage to any one. How is it that you say, 'You will be made free'" (John 8:33)?

A world devoid of absolute truth is a world filled with confusion and chaos. It shouldn't be surprising that when we remove Christianity from our culture, things become more and more disoriented, tangled, disturbing and perplexing. This untruth and deformation taking place leads individuals to claiming a kind of pseudo freedom where they develop their own truth. In a sense, we have once again eaten the forbidden fruit, buying the enchanting lie of the subtle serpent that "when you eat of it your eyes will be opened, and you will be like God, knowing good and evil" (Genesis 3:5). The sober reality is, when we disobey God, our vision becomes distorted and blurry, leading to an identity less like the God of freedom and more like the evil one eternally chained. We no longer know anything as objective. Truth? What is truth? Lost in the cosmos, without real purpose and direction, we hide from God and cling to the slavery of our bondage.

Thanks be to God, he always comes seeking us out of this condition of depravity to dispel the darkness. Again, Jesus spoke to them, saying, "I am the light of the world; he who follows me will not walk in darkness, but will have the light of life" (John 8:12).

Truth and light are united in Christ. Recalling the goal of our journey, we seek to walk out of the Purgative state and into the Illuminative state of the spiritual life, from darkness into great light. Freed from the vices that cloud our vision, God can reveal his mysteries and illuminate the mind and heart with truth and light.

"The true light that enlightens every man was coming into the world. He was in the world, and the world was made through him, yet the world knew him not. He came to his own home, and his own people received him not. But to all who received him, who believed in his name, he gave power to become children of God; who were born, not of blood nor of the will of the flesh nor of the will of man, but of God. And the Word became flesh and dwelt among us, full of grace and truth; we have beheld his glory, glory as of the only Son from the Father" (John 1:9-14).

Jesus Christ has come to illuminate the condition you find yourself in. The darker the night, the brighter the light will shine. Let us clear up the clouds that distort our vision and prepare a way for the light of the Lord. As our hearts are purified, our eyes will be opened and we will surely see God (see Matthew 5:8).

"In the presence of Christ, who is Truth itself, the truth of each man's relationship with God will be laid bare. The Last Judgment will reveal even to its furthest consequences the good each person has done or failed to do during his earthly life" (CCC 1039). As the way, the truth and the life, Jesus Christ prevails as the only way to authentic freedom.

Section 5:

The Dark Night

"No matter how much individuals do through their own efforts,
they cannot actively purify themselves enough to be disposed in the
least degree for the divine union of the perfect love. God must take
over and purge them in that fire that is dark for them."

St. John of the Cross

Day 27
Eustace and The Dragon

If you know "The Chronicles of Narnia" you have heard the story of Eustace, the troublesome cousin of Edmond, Lucy and crew. The fifth book, "The Voyage of the Dawn Treader", tells the story of how Eustace became a dragon and was turned back into a boy. Sometimes fictional stories for children can capture beautiful truths even better than theological language. Thus, the brilliance and inspiration of the great C.S. Lewis.

Everyone knows that if you walk into a dragon's lair, find a world full of insurmountable treasure, have dragonish thoughts fill your heart as it becomes consumed by the treasure, then you too will turn into a monster. Welcome to the adventures of Eustace! He fell asleep amidst all the gold and diamonds and woke up a beastly dragon.

Eustace was miserable, a real pest as a human but even more so as a dragon. He couldn't bear to glance at his own reflection and was ashamed to be around others. Once he realized that he had mutated into a monster, cut off from companionship with his friends, an overwhelming loneliness and isolation descended upon him. As the despair of becoming a dragon set in, it actually initiated the start of a transformation within Eustace. If it's possible to fathom, even in his misery he was actually a more friendly, likable, and pleasant dragon than he was a human. Nonetheless, left to himself, he would remain a dragon forever.

Then Eustace had an encounter with Aslan. It was the lion himself who came searching for Eustace (think of Aslan as the Christ-figure in the wonderful world of Narnia). Eustace did not even know Aslan yet, but his gravitational pull was irresistible. Leading the dragon up a mountain to a well full of crystal clear water, Aslan asked the dragon to "undress" which meant to take off the coat of scales, similar to how a snake would shed its skin. Let's turn to Eustace to explain what happened next:

"So I started scratching myself and my scales began coming off all over the place. And then I scratched a little deeper and, instead of just scales coming off here and there, my whole skin started peeling off beautifully...as if I was a banana...I just stepped out of it. I could see it lying there beside me, looking rather nasty. It was a most lovely feeling. So I started to go down into the well for my bath."

As Eustace began to lower his feet into the water to be cleansed he noticed all the scales covering his body once again. Assuming this to just be another inner layer, he went back to work again:

"I scratched and tore again and this underskin peeled off beautifully and I stepped and left it lying beside the other one and went down to the well for my bath. Well, exactly the same thing happened again. And I thought to myself, oh dear, how ever many skins have I got to take off?...So I scratched away for the third time and got off a third skin...and stepped out of it. But as soon as I looked at myself in the water I knew it had been no good."

My friends, is this not our precise experience on the pathway to freedom? I cannot tell you just how much I relate to poor Eustace, as his story seems to vividly sum up the drama of our human condition. Through our own decisions we became dragons, enslaved by the wretchedness of our hearts. After taking a deeper look, we quickly became ashamed at what had become of us. Then the Lord came seeking after us, offering a well of life-giving water so that we may be cleansed, restored and made whole again. He beckons us to "undress", to rid ourselves of all the sin and scales that have come to define our lives. With patience, he allows us to work hard to tear these things off and out of our lives, but the scales keep coming back. We try again and again. We believe it's gone for good and yet there it is again...that same sin! The same hardness of heart. The worst of us comes back again in those certain moments and we find ourselves back on our knees, feeling powerless.

We have labored diligently throughout this journey to make resolutions to eliminate the sin in our lives. We have been employing everything within our own power to wage war against the world, the flesh and the devil and the subsequent seven deadly sins of lust, gluttony, sloth, wrath, greed, envy and pride. But if you are anything like Eustace (and me), there are deeper layers still.

Then the lion said... "You will have to let me undress you."

"I was afraid of his claws...but I was pretty nearly desperate now. So I just lay flat down on my back to let him do it. The very first tear he made was so deep that I thought it had gone right into my heart...it hurt worse than anything I've ever felt. The only thing that made me able to bear it was just the pleasure of feeling the stuff peel off...Well, he peeled the beastly stuff right off - just as I thought I'd done it myself the other times...I started swimming and splashing and I found that all the pain had gone from my arm. And then I saw why. I'd turned into a boy again...After a bit the lion took me out and dressed me...in new clothes."

In order to be purified to the very depths of our being, we have to be desperate enough, broken enough, to lie down and allow the Lord full access. We have to give him permission to come deeply into our hearts and transform us into a new creation. Our journey will begin to take a dramatic shift as things in our control (active purgation) are released so that the Lord can take over from there (passive purgation).

As Eustace recalled this incredible encounter of transformation, he questioned Edmund, "But who is Aslan? Do you know him?" Edmund responded, "Well - he knows me...He is the great Lion...who saved me and saved Narnia. We've all seen him. Lucy sees him most often. And it may be Aslan's country we are sailing to."

The Lord saved the Israelites. He has saved men and women in every generation. He comes to set us free. After all, it is the real Promised Land that we are sailing to! You may not meet an honorable and fearless talking mouse named Reepicheep, but I promise it will be an adventure of a lifetime!

Day 28
Active and Passive Purgation

C.S. Lewis' fictional story of Eustace and the dragon represents an epic visual illustration into the reality of the two types of purification that a soul must endure: active and passive purgation. The Catechism seeks to more clearly define the distinction between the two:

"Penance...can consist of prayer, an offering, works of mercy, service of neighbor, voluntary self-denial, sacrifices, and above all the patient acceptance of the cross we must bear" (CCC 1460).

The first half of the statement could be defined as 'active' purgation highlighting prayer, offerings, works of mercy, service of neighbor, voluntary self-denial and sacrifices. This is precisely where our time has been spent thus far. As a necessity in the spiritual life, we have to do our part and willfully enter into ongoing self-denial. The good news is we have been active in our purgation specifically in context of the seven deadly sins, likely wrestling with a pretty extensive list of action items.

Over the next few days we will make a shift and focus on the second half from the Catechism or what we could call 'passive' purgation, "above all the patient acceptance of the cross we must bear." The hard work we have been putting in is required, but unfortunately it can only get us so far. Recall Eustace (as the dragon) ripping the first three layers of scales off his body and peeling off his skin only to find another deeper layer. It wasn't until he allowed Aslan to do the purging that the cleansing was fully complete.

Reflecting upon the insight from St. John of the Cross, one of the greatest masters in the spiritual life within the life of the Church, "No matter how much individuals do through their own efforts, they cannot actively purify themselves enough to be disposed in the least degree for the divine union of the perfect love. God must take over and purge them in that fire that is dark for them" (The Dark Night of the Soul, 1.3.3).

To truly be liberated out of the Purgative state and overcome our sins and vices we must allow God full access. We must allow God to take over the process.

When we submit ourselves fully, totally abandoned to the will of God, the Lord can do amazing things. Are we able to let go? Do we trust in his gentleness, compassion and mercy? Do we believe in his plan for our lives? Bottom line, how badly do we really want to be free? These are the deep-seeded questions we must ask ourselves and how we answer these questions changes everything. Up until this point we have worked hard to strengthen our will through the active works of prayer, fasting and almsgiving to be able to graciously accept the daily crosses that come our way.

The daily crosses are both big and small and the inconveniences of life still apply: difficulties at work, challenging economic times, daily traffic, annoying or non-agreeable people, physical or mental illnesses, endless medical bills, being falsely accused or constantly misunderstood, having your heart broken, being betrayed by a friend, loss of job, loss of a loved one, and so on and so forth. Life is hard. At times, the circumstances can seem almost unbearable. Passive purgation, the "patient acceptance of the cross we must bear", can carry us through our final step of the Purgative state and into the Illuminative state where we truly become a new creation in Christ. Once again, it's God initiative to bring us into true freedom and union with him.

Let us return for a moment to "The Voyage of the Dawn Treader" and reread this account based on our deeper understanding. Like Eustace, the active purgation prepares us for the passive:

Then the lion said… "You will have to let me undress you."

"I was afraid of his claws...but I was pretty nearly desperate now. So, I just lay flat down on my back to let him do it. The very first tear he made was so deep that I thought it had gone right into my heart...it hurt worse than anything I've ever felt. The only thing that made me able to bear it was just the pleasure of feeling the stuff peel off...Well, he peeled the beastly stuff right off - just as I thought I'd done it myself the other times...I started swimming and splashing [and] I found that all the pain had gone from my arm.

And then I saw why. I'd turned into a boy again...After a bit the lion took me out and dressed me...in new clothes."

Eustace was transformed from boy to dragon based on greed and selfishness. He was transformed back into a boy again only after a recognition of his utter depravity. He became contrite of heart. It was then that Aslan reached into his heart to a place so deep, unreachable for Eustace on his own. Eustace was free! In fact, more free than he was before the process even began.

God can bring a greater good out of every evil. No matter what you've done and where you've been God has the power to make all things new, including your heart:

"Fear not, stand firm, and see the salvation of the Lord, which he will work for you today...The Lord will fight for you, and you have only to be still" (Exodus 14:13-14).

Turning our hearts to God, let us spend a few moments in prayerful reflection: "Lord, I come before you empty, transparent before you. You know my heart, my holy desires, and yet you know my shortcomings, my selfishness and my brokenness. Strip me of everything that is not of you so that I can be truly free. Help me rid myself of all but love. Make me into a living flame of your love. Lord, have your way with me."

Day 29
Hidden Faults

"But who can discern his errors? Clear thou me from hidden faults"
(Psalm 19:12)

Earlier, I shared a personal confession story when I changed things up a bit, stating, "Bless me, Father for I have sinned...My predominate fault is _____." We are called to discern our faults, examine our conscience and clearly identify our areas of weakness. St. Augustine simply stated, "Know thyself." It is good that we have worked so hard. Although some modern Christians emphasize a life where we give up the striving and allow God to do everything, Catholics should recognize that it's not one or the other. It's both! Papal preacher, Fr. Cantalamessa teaches us, "...the secret for holiness, is thus the balance between...abandonment to the action of the Spirit and active, personal commitment...each aspect complements the other, with God Himself always taking the initiative" (Sober Intoxication of the Spirit, 14). Striking this balance is the goal of this process.

Nonetheless, even though we have made significant spiritual progress through our efforts of self-mastery, there are faults deep within us that remain hidden. Through our own efforts we may never understand them. Fr. Dave Pivonka describes such beautiful wisdom from French poet Leon Bloy that "there are places in our poor hearts which do not yet exist and into which suffering must enter so that they may. Suffering allows us to become more compassionate, understanding and loving. Our hearts of formed through suffering" (Spiritual Freedom, 88).

Now that's deep! Simply stated, God can work wonders in our hearts in ways that we could never accomplish on our own. There is no amount of chocolate or alcohol that you could ever give up that would transform you into a saint. Although we developed one, there exists no magical checklist of bullet points to work through to transform you into a saint. Your sanctity, freedom and the harmony of your holy desires and actions is God's initiative. Our job is to abandon ourselves to the sanctifying action of the Spirit and allow the Lord to mold us, form us and shape us. "Behold, like the clay in the potter's hand, so are you in my hand" (Jeremiah 18:6).

To be meek, yet strong; to be a humble servant, yet a leader; to listen, yet teach; to be merciful, yet just; to die to yourself, yet be fully alive; to be a source of love and joy to your family every day in the midst of a fallen world is unattainable on your own. We can't give what we don't have. We remain bankrupt without the Spirit of God guiding and illuminating us. Abandonment, properly understood, includes a full and total gift of self. It requires heroic humility, deep interior faith, unshakable confidence and radical obedience. The irony is that in abandonment, we find perfect fulfillment of our greatest desires. When we lose ourselves, we find new life. When we die to ourselves and become docile to the Holy Spirit's actions we become free. St. John the Baptist may have said it best, "He must increase, I must decrease" (John 3:30).

Let's look to a few other individuals who also understood this and lived it well.

On his way to martyrdom St. Ignatius of Antioch proclaimed, "Now I am beginning to become a true disciple...let me join the pure light...My earthly desires (the works of the flesh) have been crucified; there is no desire left in me for the things of this world. The living water (the Spirit) which speaks inside me says, "Come to the Father!"

Saint Therese insisted, "It is abandonment alone which guides me. I have no other compass" (Manuscrits Autobiographiques, 207). As her spirituality matured, St. Therese found that she was no longer driven by her own desires. The two competing compasses of her past had been reduced to one: doing the will of God.

St. John of the Cross began his timeless spiritual classic, "The Dark Night of the Soul", professing, "One dark night, fired by love's urgent longings - ah, the sheer grace!" Through the pain, the trials and ultimately the cross, the grace of God leads us to union and freedom. His grace is sufficient. Nothing else even compares to what our hearts experience when united fully to God.

Filled with the Holy Spirit, St. Paul pulls all of this together most perfectly, "Indeed I count everything as loss because of the surpassing worth of knowing Christ Jesus my Lord. For his sake, I have suffered the loss of all things, and count them as refuse, in order that I may gain Christ and be found in him...that I may know him and the power of his resurrection, and may share his sufferings, becoming like him in his death, that if possible I may attain the resurrection from the dead. Not that I have already obtained this or am already perfect; but I press on to make it my own, because Christ Jesus has made me his own...forgetting what lies behind and straining forward to what lies ahead, I press on toward the goal for the prize of the upward call of God in Christ Jesus" (Philippians 4:8-14).

St. Paul understood the human condition well, knowing exactly what would hold us back. He responded by passionately persuading us toward the truth, professing "I consider that the sufferings of this present time are not worth comparing with the glory that is to be revealed to us" (Romans 8:18).

To reach the Promised Land, our hidden faults must undergo the passive purgation of suffering. For St. Ignatius, the earthly desires were eliminated completely. St. Therese's only compass was abandonment to God's will. St. John of the Cross called his purgation "the dark night of the soul." St. Paul "suffered the loss of all things." These beautiful souls and countless others throughout the ages have passed through the Purgative state to delight in the "sheer grace" of God. They beckon us to join them on this great adventure back to heart of the Father. "If you allow yourself to be still, you will be able to hear and feel his beating heart. Then, as a baby finds comfort on the chest of her mother, so you will find, in the Father's heart, freedom" (Fr. Dave Pivonka, Spiritual Freedom, 93).

Day 30
Intoxication of the Spirit

The Spirit of God, which helped form and bring life into the world (see Genesis 1:2), which led Moses and the Israelites out of bondage through cloud and fire (see Exodus 13:21), which brought life to the valley of dry bones (see Ezekial 37), which overshadowed Mary to conceive the Christ-child (see Luke 1:35), which Jesus breathed on the apostles after the resurrection (see John 20:22), which appeared as tongues of fire at Pentecost (see Acts 2:4), which animated the words and actions of John the Baptist (see Luke 1:15), Elizabeth (see Luke 1:41), Zechariah (see Luke 1:67), Peter (see Acts 4:8), Paul (see Acts 9:17 or Acts 13:9), and all the disciples (see Acts 13:52), is the Spirit of Freedom!

St. Paul couldn't be more clear, "Where the Spirit of the Lord is, there is freedom" (2 Corinthians 3:17). To live an authentic Christian life of freedom without an intimate relationship with the Holy Spirit is unobtainable; fool's gold. Everything we have been traversing towards goes hand-in-hand with this reality. "And those who belong to Christ Jesus have crucified the flesh with its passions and desires. If we live by the Spirit, let us also walk by the Spirit" (Galatians 5:24-25). For "if you live according to the flesh you will die, but if by the Spirit you put to death the deeds of the body you will live" (Romans 8:13).

We have committed to wandering through our own wilderness with a definitive purpose; to mortify our passions, put to death our selfishness through charity and enter into a prayerful conversation with God every day. "As in the days of Elijah (see 1 Kings 18:38), the fire that comes down from heaven only falls on the wood the is prepared for burning!" (Sober Intoxication of the Spirit, 12). For the last thirty days, we have been preparing "the wood" of our hearts which now stands ready to be set aflame by that Holy Fire that comes down from heaven!

The greatest news is that all we have to do is come before our Heavenly Father with sincerity and ask. It's the greatest petition we could ever ask for, the one we need the most, and yet it's the one we ask for the very least. The Father longs to pour out his Spirit upon you! "If you then, who are evil, know how to give good gifts to your children, how much more will the heavenly Father give the Holy Spirit to those who ask him!" (Luke 11:13).

Filled with the Holy Spirit and purged of our selfishness, we begin to experience a freedom this world cannot offer or even imagine. We have done well to walk this narrow path through the wilderness to reach the Promised Land. Our bondage and slavery have been broken and destroyed, a thing of the past. We are now a new creation in Christ. St. Augustine reveals that "only the state of a man who has drunk so much as to lose his mind can give us an idea - even though a negative one - of what happens to the human mind when it receives the ineffable joy of the Holy Spirit...becoming intoxicated with the abundance in the house of God...tasting something of the goodness that is to come in the heavenly Jerusalem" (Commentary on the Psalms). Truly, as we continue on our journey we should began to experience glimpses and even a foretaste of paradise.

One of great spiritual fathers of our times, Fr. Cantalamessa explains, "When spiritually intoxicated, a person is out of his mind not because he is bereft of reason...but because he passes beyond reason into the light of God" (Sober Intoxication of the Spirit, 4-5).

Beyond human reason and into the light of God; this is precisely our goal! Freed from our vices and filled with the Holy Spirit, God begins to reveal his mysteries into our hearts and illuminate our minds. Our journey is nearing its destination and we can see a new light at the end of the tunnel as we pass from the Purgative state and into the Illuminative state.

Section 6:

Liberation

"In this new state, as one liberated from a cramped prison cell, it goes about the things of God with much more freedom and satisfaction of spirit and with more abundant interior delight...The soul readily finds...a very serene, loving contemplation and spiritual delight."

St. John of the Cross

Day 31
Free Indeed

After forty long years of wandering through the wilderness, the Israelites entered the Promised Land as the Lord has promised. "...the Lord said to Joshua... "Arise, go over this Jordan, you and all this people, into the land which I am giving to them, to the people of Israel. Every place that the sole of your foot will tread upon I have given to you, as I promised to Moses" (Joshua 1:1-3).

This, my friends, is the ultimate sign of freedom. Where every place you step foot is yours! Southwest Airlines understood this well with their famous slogan, "You are now free to move about the country." The Israelites were free! Free from Pharaoh and the Egyptian captivity. Free from the wilderness. And now free to move about in wide open space, worship and live the lives they always desired in the depths of their hearts.

As part of their newfound independence, the Lord was steadily teaching and guiding them. Yes, freedom is yours but now what? What will you do with your freedom? How do you remain in your freedom? What does it mean to be free?

"Be strong and very courageous, being careful to do according to all the law which Moses my servant commanded you; turn not from it to the right hand or to the left, that you may have good success wherever you go. This book of the law shall not depart out of your mouth, but you shall meditate on it day and night, that you may be careful to do according to all that is written in it; for then you shall make your way prosperous, and then you shall have good success" (Joshua 1:7-8).

In essence, the Lord is telling us, "You are free, but here are some tips to persevere and thrive, to be prosperous and have success." St. Paul says something similar but using different words, "Stand fast therefore, and do not submit again to a yoke of slavery" (Galatians 5:1).

You have worked so hard to reach this point in your spiritual life. Not only that, the Lord has been relentlessly determined to help you get here. He literally gave up his life and died for it. He rescued us at the Cross and continues to rescue us now. Free indeed, Paul beckons us not to go back into bondage!

To illustrate Paul's plea to the Galatians, I'm reminded of the scene where the Lord rescues the woman caught in the act of adultery (see John 8:4). First of all, imagine the shame of being caught "in the act." Shame quickly turned to impending death as they stood ready to stone her. Then Jesus broke into the scene, "...he stood up and said to them, "Let him who is without sin among you be the first to throw a stone at her" (John 8:7). I love this! Let's not miss the beautiful subtleties of scripture. Jesus *stands up* to the accuser on our behalf. The evangelist (John) continues this theme in the book of Revelation, "And I heard a loud voice in heaven, saying, "Now the salvation and the power and the kingdom of our God and the authority of his Christ have come, for the accuser of our brethren has been thrown down, who accuses them day and night before our God" (Revelation 12:10).

Returning to the story of the woman in shame, "And once more he bent down and wrote with his finger on the ground" (John 8:8). Many have pondered what Jesus wrote in the sand, speculating he wrote but one simple word, "Mercy".

This entire road we have been traveling has been a continuous initiative of God's infinite mercy. It was true for the Israelites. It was true for the woman caught in the act. And it's true for you and me. Our God fights for us and he forgives. So back to our questions: what will you do with your freedom? How do you remain in your freedom? What does it mean to be free?

We close with the final words of Our Lord to the accused woman, "Woman, where are they? Has no one condemned you?" She said, "No one, Lord." And Jesus said, "Neither do I condemn you; go, and do not sin again" (John 8:10-11).

Day 32
Into Great Light

During my college days, I received a unique audio CD featuring the voice of Pope John Paul II that included a mixture of prayers and music in various languages. Although only affluent in English, I just love hearing his voice. On one occasion, JPII quotes a passage from John, "Every one who does wrong hates the light, and avoids it, for fear his actions should be exposed. But the man who lives by truth comes out into the light, so that it may be clearly seen that what he does is done in God (John 3:20-21).

My friends, this is exactly what we have set out to accomplish. Our journey into great freedom is a journey into great light. God illuminates our eyes to experience a new perspective – his perspective. Sin has lost its power and death has lost its sting (see 1 Corinthians 15:55). We have sought to put to death the disordered desires and persistent passions within us and diminish the gravitational pull towards the flesh, the world and the devil. It's now time to come out of the shadows and into the freedom of the sons and daughters of God!

St. John of the Cross likens this transition in the spiritual life of coming out of the Purgative state and into the Illuminative state as a prison-break, "In this new state, as one liberated from a cramped prison cell, it goes about the things of God with much more freedom and satisfaction of spirit and with more abundant interior delight...The soul readily finds...a very serene, loving contemplation and spiritual delight" (The Dark Night of the Soul, 11.20.4).

Gaining wisdom from our ancestors, let us not spend forty years lost in the darkness of sin like the Israelites did! Through the grace and power of the Cross, we seek to break out of our self-inflicted prison much quicker. I don't suggest that you or I will never sin again, but what I do put forward is that we grow daily in freedom. That the power of sin does not overwhelm us and keep us in bondage. That we live in the light and freedom of God, free to choose right over wrong and take back control of our passions. That we allow the Spirit of God to guide our hearts and restore our minds with a new sense of clarity. As the scales of our sin are reduced and obliterated, our darkened intellect and weakened will shall experience an absolute and outright transformation, culminating with a satisfying inner harmony and perpetual peace that can only come from the living God. Disorder returns to order. Shame is converted into holy audacity and humble confidence in the Lord. Fear is replaced by unshakable trust.

Some give in to the temptation that the Illuminative state is not for them but only the super-holy souls like nuns, priests or deacons, apathetically believing that they will never truly rid themselves of their sins or addictions, so why even try. Let us expose any of these clouded thought processes to the light, and let God's illuminating power shine on every corner of our lives until the lies are burned away.

Emptied out from the toils of our holy expedition, let us bask in the light of Christ and allow the warmth of his light to dispel away any darkness that remains.

- "O house of Jacob, come, let us walk in the light of the Lord" (Isaiah 2:5).
- "The people who walked in darkness have seen a great light; those who dwelt in a land of deep darkness, on them has light shined" (Isaiah 9:2).
- "I am the light of the world; he who follows me will not walk in darkness, but will have the light of life" (John 8:12).
- "This is the message we have heard from him and proclaim to you, that God is light and in him is no darkness at all. If we say we have fellowship with him while we walk in darkness, we lie and do not live according to the truth; but if we walk in the light, as he is in the light, we have fellowship with one another, and the blood of Jesus his Son cleanses us from all sin" (1 John 1:5-8).
- "The light shines in the darkness, and the darkness has not overcome it...The true light that enlightens every man was coming into the world" (John 1:5-9).

Day 33
Ease and Joy

Have you ever watched Stephen Curry (NBA All-Star) shoot a long range three-pointer and it just beautifully splash through the net without even touching the rim? Or notice how he dances around his helpless defender and then (effortlessly) pulls back for a 30-foot rainmaker? As a son of a life-long basketball coach who spent hours upon hours in the driveway practicing every day, watching Mr. Curry perfect his trade with such ease is just a beautiful thing to witness. He has already put in the work behind the scenes, investing countless hours refining his craft. At this point in his career, hoisting up a seemingly half-court shot is accomplished with ease and joy. Extreme muscle memory has been acquired through practice, allowing for the distance and precision to become second nature to him.

This analogy isn't perfect of course but it's not entirely unlike the spiritual life. The Purgative state can be grueling at times. It's hard work. A real death in ourselves takes place as we mortify our passions and desires to kill the disorder and selfishness within. We accept the daily crosses that come our way, dealing with the pain, sorrow, loss, sin, consequences of sin, setbacks, loss of friends, hardships and even persecution for our Christian faith. But over time the selfishness begins to die and the light of God brings with it a certain ease and joy about things.

When you do something over and over a habit forms, albeit good or bad. Actions that become habitually bad the Church calls vices; those habitually good we call virtues. Once a habit emerges into a virtue, the soul performs it with ease and joy! It's no longer tedious and laborious. The grind that we undertake and the mortification that we put ourselves through has an end in mind...freedom and communion with divine love.

"Human virtues are firm attitudes, stable dispositions, habitual perfections of intellect and will that govern our actions, order our passions, and guide our conduct according to reason and faith. They make possible ease, self-mastery, and joy in leading a morally good life. The virtuous man is he who freely practices the good. The

110

moral virtues are acquired by human effort. They are the fruit and seed of morally good acts; they dispose all the powers of the human being for communion with divine love" (CCC 1804).

When a soul begins the spiritual war against the flesh, the world, and the devil it has to work extremely hard to put forth the effort required. There is no way to shortchange the toil we went through along the journey so far. Upon reaching the Illuminative state things start to change and there is a much greater satisfaction and delight in the Spirit.

When you first choose to begin acting with humility in everything you do it may seem difficult, but eventually a joyful, humble soul arises. When you deliberately deny yourself through fasting, moderation starts becoming quite easy. As distractions are removed and replaced with firm resolutions for daily prayer, over time prayer becomes your favorite time of the day. A soul can truly and authentically become charitable, faithful, meek and pure of heart. In a word, a soul can become selfless, capable of being accomplished with great peace, ease and joy. This is a peace and joy the world simply cannot give, the state of grace that only comes from God and freely offered for each and every soul he has created.

"Human virtues [are] acquired...by deliberate acts and by a perseverance ever-renewed in repeated efforts are purified and elevated by divine grace. With God's help, they forge character and give facility in the practice of the good. The virtuous man is happy to practice them" (CCC 1810).

The human person is drawn to beauty with every experience of beauty pointing to infinity. This compelling power of the beautiful ultimately leads to truth. Therefore, many have said that it's beauty itself that will transform the world.

Today we end with the following from Fr. Thomas Dubay, "Those who faithfully practice all the virtues, those patient through persecution, with purity of heart in a lust-filled society, those with a selfless and burning love for God and neighbor...A heroically holy man or woman is the pinnacle of visible creation. The saintly reach a splendor and beauty beyond all comparison. Selfless love is a reflection of the divine artist in action" (The Evidential Power of Beauty).

Go...be free and bring beauty into the world. May the light of his grace shine through you and be expressed in grace-filled virtue. Nothing is more beautiful!

Day 34
A New Creation

When she's not taking care of our four children (five if you count me), my wife is an author and speaker who travels around the country proclaiming the good news of the gospel. Young girls frequently approach her after her talks clarifying, "Really, you mean to say that in Christ I can genuinely be made new? She always responds, "Yes, that's what I'm saying: A new creation! Christ can make you a new creation!"

St. Paul himself experienced a brand-new life, "It is no longer I who live, but Christ who lives in me" (Galatians 2:20). In the case of Simon (Peter), his life was so profoundly new that Christ even changed his name in the process!

Satan tempts us into sin by tricking us into justifying it, "It's not that bad; it won't harm anyone. This is actually an act of love not a sin...and so on." Later, when seeking forgiveness with the Lord, he tempts us in the exact opposite way, "But your sin is too great. You are damaged goods and no longer pure. Did you forget about that sin you committed thirty years ago...that one was just horrible, nobody knows about that one," and so on.

Remember, the devil lies because he is envious. He knows the truth will set us free and strives to keep us from it! Contrarily, the Holy Spirit, the Spirit of truth speaking through St. Paul proclaims, "Therefore, if anyone is in Christ, he is a new creation; the old has passed away, behold, the new has come (2 Corinthians 5:17). Everything about the New Testament signifies this reality. We encounter a new Exodus story, a new Moses, a new creation story, a new Adam, a new Eve, a new tree of life, a new manna from Heaven and a new birth into the life of grace.

Nicodemus famously questioned how this is possible to be made new again, "How can a man be born when he is old? Can he enter a second time into his mother's womb and be born?" Jesus answered, "Truly, truly, I say to you...That which is born of the flesh is flesh, and that which is born of the Spirit is spirit. Do not marvel that I said to you, 'You must be born anew'" (John 3:4-7).

In addition to Baptism, there is also a rebirth in the Spirit of God that takes place. Our journey out of bondage through the wilderness and into a life in the Spirit is this rebirth. We call upon the spirit of God daily to make us anew through his mercy. Even creation testifies of this resurrection, as the sun arises anew each day. Today is a new day, exploding with endless possibilities and opportunities to grow in love for God and neighbor. Today is a new day of freedom!

"As far as the east is from the west, so far does he remove our transgressions from us." (Psalm 103:12). He has blotted them out. He remembers them no more. Consider yourself a new creation in Christ! Let this truth penetrate to the depths of your being.

"All this is from God, who through Christ reconciled us to himself and gave us the ministry of reconciliation; that is, God was in Christ reconciling the world to himself, not counting their trespasses against them, and entrusting to us the message of reconciliation" (2 Corinthians 5:18-19).

"And he who sat upon the throne said, "Behold, I make all things new" (Revelation 21:5).

Day 35
The Fruit of the Spirit

My wife and I are blessed to have four beautiful children. We have always marveled at how together with God, we can bring life into the world. There is something uniquely mind-blowing when it is your own child being formed in the womb; though ironically, this reality remains hidden for several weeks while mother and father have no idea that the child is even present there.

How do you know when you are free? How do you know that the Spirit of God, the Spirit of Freedom is dwelling within you? It's interesting that right when St. Paul starts talking about the nature of Christian freedom, he calls our attention to the fruit of the Spirit:

"But the fruit of the Spirit is love, joy, peace, patience, kindness, goodness, faithfulness, gentleness, self-control; against such there is no law. And those who belong to Christ Jesus have crucified the flesh with its passions and desires" (Galatians 5:22-24).

Are you filled with love? Would others, especially those closest to you, describe you as joyful? Does the peace of Christ guard your mind and heart and bring peace to others? Are you patient with others: with God, your spouse, your children, your co-workers, with traffic? Are you gracious and kind to others even when you don't get your way? Do you go about the day filled with goodness even seeing the goodness of God in others? Are you faithful to God, your spouse, your prayer life, your children, your friends and your job? Do you treat others with gentleness and compassion, genuinely listening and caring for their needs? Do you have self-control over your actions, words and passions?

Christ taught us that as you grow in freedom the fruit becomes tangible, explaining, "You will know them by their fruits" (Matthew 7:16). Thus, our reflection on the fruits of the Spirit can help ground us when trying to understand our own spiritual lives as well as the struggles faced by others. Someone may think they are "on fire" and walking with the Lord, but fall significantly short on love, joy, peace...and so on. Conversely, another may feel as though they have lost the Spirit or don't get the same satisfaction of the Spirit, while still being the most loving, joyful, peaceful, kind, good, faithful, gentle, and self-mastered person you have ever met. At the end of the day, if we live in the Spirit, our lives should bear the fruit of the Spirit. There are certainly mountains and valleys in life that affect our human feelings and emotions, but the fruits of the spirit remain.

We've all tried to pull ourselves up by our bootstraps and decide that we are, by our own merit, capable of possessing these fruits of the Spirit. I have tried to decide to be joyful. I have tried to decide to have patience or self-control. However, while this may work for a few days (or in some cases, a few minutes!), we find ourselves unable to master these fruits on our own. If it were possible, then surely we would all choose to exercise them always.

Continuing with Christ's message, "A sound tree cannot bear evil fruit, nor can a bad tree bear good fruit. Every tree that does not bear good fruit is cut down and thrown into the fire" (Matthew 7:18-19). A tree is only as stable as the depths of its roots. If we want to be strong, able to weather the storms of life and bear the fruits of the Spirit, our roots must reach deep enough to drink of the Spirit himself. If you are struggling with one of these fruits, don't look at the exterior branches for your answers. You will only find what you are looking for by reaching deeper. Allow your roots to sink into the depths to draw from the living water of the Holy Spirit.

"Blessed is the man who...delights in the law of the LORD, and on his law he meditates day and night. He is like a tree planted by streams of water, that yields its fruit in its season, and its leaf does not wither. In all that he does, he prospers" (Psalm 1:3).

116

Section 7:

Three-Fold Expression of Freedom

"The more one does what is good, the freer one becomes...By the working of grace the Holy Spirit educates us in spiritual freedom in order to make us free collaborators in his work in the Church and in the world."

Catechism of the Catholic Church
1733-1742

Day 36
Abiding Presence

Freedom is not just what we are freed from, but also what we are freed for. We are set free from the bondage of sin for a life of superabundance, to live as sons of the Father and heirs to his kingdom. We are set free to become fully human, fully ourselves and fully alive in all that God has created us to be. Ultimately, we are set free to give ourselves away, just as Christ did on the Cross. To be fully alive is to be fully given!

To understand how to express our freedom, we will turn to Christ who was so free that he could even freely choose to lay down his life for us. Our three-fold expression of freedom will consist of abiding presence, joyful service and loving sacrifice, contemplating each of these in more detail over the next three days.

My brother and I are best friends. We have always enjoyed spending time together, conversing about a variety of topics ranging from deep theological truths to debates over the best current NBA superstar. I still remember one of those life conversations a few years back regarding his work/life balance.

After racing past his wife and kids again to dash straight into his office to continue the work of the day, his wife sat him down. In essence, she told him that if you are going be on a work call just don't come home until you are finished. It sends a message to the children that work is more important than they are. Yikes! As you might expect, that hit him square between the eyes and that's when he called to chat. We talked for a while and formulated a simple resolution – before you get out of the car each day, decide what kind of husband and father you are going to be before you walk through that door. This was one of the original seeds that God planted in my heart that eventually led to writing and producing "The Door - The Power of Presence" (https://youtu.be/gza0eHz1snY).

The Door is a short film that enters into a daily decision point for men. It shows the dynamic impact a father can make to his entire family with a simple choice. The video reminds men of their incredible vocations as husbands and fathers called to bring joy into their homes.

Good men, who sacrifice and work so hard to provide for their families, are faced with what has been called "the daily drama of fatherhood." These are good men who love God and their families with all their heart. On one hand, men are called to be providers; on the other hand, a man's loving presence and relationships with his wife and children are irreplaceable. Between these two great callings exists a daily tension that so many modern men face.

At the depths of our identity as men, we are both sons and fathers. Saint John Paul II proclaimed that men are called to reveal and relive on earth the very fatherhood of God. Now that is some pretty deep stuff. I really believe the video touches this depth, this sacred place within the heart of each man, whether he knows it or not. Like God the Father, our love for our children is unconditional. We would give them anything, right!? Sometimes we just need to be reminded that they need our time; they need our friendship. A good friend sent me a text message recently with the simplest of truths, "Children spell love…T-I-M-E."

Diving even deeper, if men are called to reflect the very fatherhood of God then we ought to contemplate the mystery of God. While every other religion on earth is man seeking God, with Christianity we know it to be the exact opposite. Our God comes seeking after us! He passionately pursues us, "And the Word became flesh and dwelt among us" (John 1:14). In the Incarnation, the Lord leaves his world behind, foregoing his throne in the heavens to make a true descent. He comes down to our level, but doesn't stop there, "This man receives sinners and eats with them" (Luke 15:2). Our God meets us wherever we are – saint or sinner. He enters into our sorrow and cares deeply for our souls, as intimate as he is infinite. "And when he drew near and saw the city he wept over it" (Luke 19:41). And we all know how the story ends, freely laying down his life for us at the Cross, "No one takes it from me, but I lay it down of my own accord. I have the power to lay it down, and I have the power to take it again…" (John 10:18).

So here is the million-dollar question: Why? Why does God go to such extremes? My proposal to you is simply this: To give us his abiding presence. The Father has an infinite desire to be with his children. The gift of Creation, the gift of the Incarnation and the gift of Heaven itself are all gifts of his presence. In his infinite goodness, he even offers his presence *within* us through the gifts of

119

Baptism, the Eucharist and the Holy Spirit. This is the all-consuming desire of the Father!

God's abiding presence is the most powerful force in the world. Brothers and sisters, your abiding presence in your home, if lived well, has the potential to bring with it the same power because as Saint John Paul II so eloquently proclaimed, "The future of the world and of the church passes through the family" (Familiaris Consortio, 75). Imagine millions of fathers and mothers spending more time with their children, bringing the love, peace and joy of the Lord into their homes. It's this love that literally brings life into the world and sustains our existence. Our freedom is meant to be used to love...freely. It's really this simple, God wants *your* family to experience more joy. More smiles, more laughter and a life filled with superabundant joy.

As we walk through the door each day we have a definitive decision point. In literally the first ten seconds, what kind of person are we going to be? Pope Francis has asked parents on multiple occasions to "waste time with their children." Do you waste time with your children? Do you waste time with your spouse? Or...do you waste time on technology, vain pursuits or the things of this world that are passing away?

In our freedom, we must make a daily descent into the lives of our loved ones. Like God, we must leave our world of work, personal pursuits and agendas joyfully and willingly and enter into the lives of others. We are called to an intimacy with them; we are called into a communion of persons.

How you spend your time is how you spend yourself. Resolve to bring joy to others, starting first and foremost in your own home. This is one decision I promise you will never regret.

Day 37
Joyful Service

As two of the greatest evangelists in the history of Christianity, the lives of St. Peter and St. Paul cannot be understated. Both men encountered Our Lord in radically different ways and left everything behind to follow him. Both were martyred in Rome, Peter crucified upside down while Paul was sentenced to a beheading. These two heroic apostles of Our Lord have something very specific to remind us about this journey into freedom we have been embarking upon.

St. Peter exhorts us, "Live as free men, yet without using your freedom as a pretext for evil; but live as servants of God" (1 Peter 2:16). Peter very clearly illustrates the appropriate expression of our Christian freedom. When we fully possess ourselves, we can make a free choice to serve God.

Inspired by the same Holy Spirit, St. Paul's message echoes a similar tone, "For you were called to freedom, brethren; only do not use your freedom as an opportunity for the flesh, but through love be servants of one another" (Galatians 5:13). Once again freedom and service are connected. Our freedom is clearly demonstrated and expressed through service.

Notice the subtle difference between the two statements — Peter calls upon us to be servants of God, while Paul asks us to be servants of one another. This is an absolutely beautiful working of the Holy Spirit because between the two of them they have fully understood and reiterated the two greatest commandments Christ taught us, "You shall love the Lord your God with all your heart, and with all your soul, and with all your mind. This is the great and first commandment. And a second is like it, You shall love your neighbor as yourself. On these two commandments depend all the law and the prophets" (Matthew 22:37-40).

To love and serve both God and our neighbor, this is our Christian calling! Furthermore, Christ taught us how to love another person by laying down our life for them. "Greater love has no man than this, that a man lay down his life for his friends" (John 15:13).

Finally, let us remember that our service to God and others is called to be filled with joy...especially when it is most difficult. In fact, this is the very first instruction St. James imparts upon us, "Count it all joy, my brethren, when you meet various trials, for you know that the testing of your faith produces steadfastness. And let steadfastness have its full effect, that you may be perfect and complete, lacking in nothing" (James 1:2-4).

Day 38
Loving Sacrifice

When I think of love, I think of the Cross. When I think of sacrifice, of excruciating pain, of what it means to be Christian, I think of the Cross. When I think of joy, I think of the Resurrection...which only came by virtue of the Cross.

Some segments of modern Christianity tend to focus primarily on the joys and blessings of knowing and loving Jesus. We have all heard of the so-called gospel of prosperity, aka the 'health and wealth' gospel. I certainly believe that God desires to bring us a joy that this world cannot offer. What father does not want to bring joy and happiness to his beloved?

While all this is absolutely true, there is more to the story and more depth to the message of the gospel. The Lord loves us so much that he bestows upon us the dignity, as mere humans, to enter into his mystery and follow him to live the very life that he lived. What do I mean by that? Well, he allows us to endure crosses and resurrections. He allows us to freely choose these sacrifices. And through the grace of his Cross and Resurrection, he gives power to ours so that our sacrificial lives may be redemptive to others as well. We do not become *the* Redeemer, but we do become cooperators with the Redeemer. When we offer our sacrifices and sufferings in union with the grace of the Cross, they are given divine power. I want us to hear this loud and clear—we are given divine power! Our lives can become immersed in the mystery of redemption.

Consider these somewhat scandalizing words of St. Paul, "Now I rejoice in my sufferings for your sake, and in my flesh I complete what is lacking in Christ's afflictions for the sake of his body, that is, the church..." (Colossians 1:24). Is Paul saying Christ did not suffer enough? What exactly is lacking?

Brothers and sisters, what is lacking in Christ's afflictions is our participation in them! Christ paid the price once and for all, but he calls upon us to follow him along the way, to live the life he lived. To be a Christian is to be a "little" Christ. There is no Christianity without the Cross.

In the Beatitudes, Jesus reveals to us the ultimate guide to the depths of an authentically Christian life. Described by many as Christ's greatest teaching, the Beatitudes progress in the order in which they are proclaimed. For example, the first Beatitude is blessed are the "poor in spirit", signifying that the spiritual life begins with humility. So where do the Beatitudes end? "Blessed are those who are persecuted for righteousness' sake, for theirs is the kingdom of heaven. Blessed are you when men revile you and persecute you and utter all kinds of evil against you falsely on my account. Rejoice and be glad, for your reward is great in heaven, for so men persecuted the prophets who were before you" (Matthew 5:10-12).

St. Paul embraced this fully and with such freedom that he could even rejoice in his own sufferings for the sake of others. He embraced it so fully that he could say, "I have been crucified with Christ; it is no longer I who live, but Christ who lives in me..." (Galatians 2:20).

When Christ lives in us it is his light that will shine through us. Pain and suffering will still come our way, but upon arriving at the Illuminative or Unitive state our hearts now have the eyes to see the redemptive value. Perspectives begin changing, leading to deeper contemplation into the sublime mysteries and wisdom of God. Like Christ (and St. Paul), you yourself become an offering for others. You have become another Christ...a Christian.

When we gaze into a stained-glass window we see and experience the beauty and splendor of the Saints. What we are really seeing is the light from the sun shine through the multi-colored glass. The glass allows the sun to shine through it. His light must become our light. His life must become our life.

May our freedom be expressed in loving sacrifice. In doing so, we become like God himself as we partake in his divine nature and power. His love, lived through us, can transform the world:

"His divine power has granted to us all things that pertain to life and godliness, through the knowledge of him who called us to his own glory and excellence, by which he has granted to us his precious and very great promises, that through these you may escape from the corruption that is in the world because of passion, and become partakers of the divine nature" (2 Peter 1:3-4).

Section 8:

The Promised Land

"This step of love causes the soul to burn gently...The Holy Spirit produces this gentle and delightful ardor by reason of the perfect soul's union with God. We cannot speak of the goods and riches of God a person enjoys on this step because even were we to write many books about them the greater part would remain unsaid."

St. John of the Cross

Day 39
The Paradise of God

The Hebrew term for 'heaven' or 'paradise' is 'Gan Eden'. From the very beginning, Adam and Eve were placed in a type of paradise. The garden of Eden was a paradise of pleasure. Together, man and woman enjoyed both communion with God and communion with one another. When sin entered the world, everything changed. Man was driven out of the paradise of the garden and God "placed the cherubim, and a flaming sword which turned every way, to guard the way to the tree of life" (Genesis 3:24). Paradise was lost and humanity was incapable of returning on its own accord.

The New Testament is a recapitulation of the Fall. Christ, the new Adam (see 1 Corinthians 15:45) is once again tempted in the garden (Gethsemane), and once again present with the woman (Mary, the new Eve) at the Tree of Life (the Cross). Christ was crucified, placed in a tomb and risen from the dead in a garden (see John 19:41). Later Mary Magdalene encounters the Resurrected Christ and supposed him to be...you guessed it...the gardener (see John 20:15). The new fruit from the new tree of life in the new garden is none other than the Eucharist. What Adam lost, Christ restored. Satan's apparent victory is left turned on its head.

Let's go further still, "...one of the soldiers pierced his side with a spear, and at once there came out blood and water...For these things took place that the scripture might be fulfilled..." (John 19:34-36). In Eden, God placed a heavenly guardian with a flaming sword to block paradise, preventing its re-entry. At the Cross, all of salvation history is fulfilled at precisely the moment an earthly soldier pierces the heart of Christ with a sword. With the opening of Christ's heart, paradise is restored. Through the wounded heart of the Savior, we once again have access to the Paradise of God. To enter into Paradise is to enter into the heart of God. Or rather, to enter into the heart of God is to enter into Paradise. His blood has paid the ransom for our sins and the water has cleansed us and made us new. The wounded and pierced heart of Christ serves as the open door to our salvation "which no one is able to shut" (Revelation 3:8).

126

Although we've sinned, turned from God and succumbed to the temptations and subtleties of the devil, God had a plan to restore what was lost. The entire biblical account represents a journey back into union with God. It's an adventure back into the heart of the Father where we find his efficacious and lasting freedom. It's a journey back into the Paradise of God. And it's God himself who comes to our rescue and fights relentlessly on our behalf.

"The whole of the Christian life is like a great pilgrimage to the house of the Father, whose unconditional love for every human creature, and in particular for the 'prodigal son'...should encourage everyone to undertake...a journey of conversion" (Saint John Paul II). On the vigil of Divine Mercy Sunday, 2005, the Pope uttered his final audible words, "Let me go to my Father's house."

Our journey out of bondage and into the Promised Land is a mission to find ultimate (and splendid!) union with God. Our forty days is but a start along the journey of a lifetime, or as the Franciscans like to say, "continual conversion." The omnipotent, omniscient and immutable God, the Alpha and Omega, the transcendent One, the Creator, the Redeemer and the Sanctifier, allows his heart to be wounded, crushed and opened. He descends into the depth of the human condition to elevate us into the heights of his Trinitarian life and love. He longs to restore us to himself, bringing about union with his people. Our God is the Father who wants to share all that he is and all that he has with his sons and daughters.

The three defining factors of Heaven are as follows:

1. Being in the presence and/or union with God.
2. There is no sin. Heaven and sin are mutually exclusive. They cannot exist together.
3. No more suffering (see Revelation 21:4).

The last of the three states of the spiritual life is the Unitive state. It's true that the ultimate union with God takes place only when a soul reaches Heaven itself, the eschatological promised land. Nonetheless, some souls reach and experience a type of heavenly union even during their life on Earth. Radiating the love of Christ to all they encounter, the great Saints were so closely united to God and consumed with his love that they became a living flame of love. Everything else was burned away and purified. Every action, every word, every movement becomes motivated by love alone. "[This] step of love causes the soul to burn gently...The Holy Spirit produces this gentle and delightful ardor by reason of the perfect soul's union with God. We cannot speak of the goods and riches of God a person enjoys on this step because even were we to write many books about them the greater part would remain unsaid" (The Dark Night of the Soul, II.20.4).

Day 40
I Thirst

"Jesus, knowing that all was now finished, said (to fulfill the scripture), "I thirst" (John 19:28).

Jesus refused offers to satiate his physical thirst on multiple occasions throughout his passion. Reaching much deeper beyond the mere physical thirst, his final words reveal a consummate thirst to bring us back into communion with the Father. And yet his thirst goes even deeper.

The thirst of the Son is to return to the Father. Jesus' heart was (and is) completely and eternally consumed with a burning love for God the Father. Before the foundation of the world, this very love existed, "begetting" the Holy Spirit in its fruitfulness. It's precisely out of this love that creation formed into existence. Out of this love, humanity is created in his image and the Redeemer is sent to save us. Out of this love, he freely carried his cross to Calvary and planted the new tree of life, destroying death itself once and for all. Out of this love, the gates of Paradise are now opened wide for all souls. It's a love that transcends beyond the grave, to the very end...and beyond. It cannot be destroyed; it always overcomes... every situation!

Indeed, Jesus died of thirst, stretching out his entire being to the end of love. With an infinite desire in his heart for union with the Father, nothing would ultimately separate him from this longing. Nothing could reduce, steal, or satiate this unquenchable thirst.

For this reason, we end our journey precisely where we began, seeking to ignite "A Heart on Fire with Desire." We aspire to end this earthly pilgrimage inflamed with a burning desire in our hearts for union with God the Father. In other words, my greatest prayer for you is that, like our Lord, you would die of thirst. That the desire and thirst in your heart would be continually enkindled and grow from a faint flicker to an intoxicating flame of love. This is precisely why Our Lord pursues us, "I came to cast fire upon the earth; and would that it were already kindled!" (Luke 12:49).

Over the course of this incredible journey we have come to know our enemies. We have encountered them head-on, understanding the powers and forces that seek to reduce us into bondage, steal our joy and holy desires and reckon us less human. To preserve in our journey towards Heaven we must not only persevere in faith, virtue and good works, but always retain our first love. Once again, it a matter of the heart.

"I know your works, your toil and your patient endurance, and how you cannot bear evil men but have tested those who call themselves apostles but are not, and found them to be false; I know you are enduring patiently and bearing up for my name's sake, and you have not grown weary. But I have this against you, that you have abandoned the love you had at first. Remember then from what you have fallen, repent and do the works you did at first" (Revelations 2:2-5).

In Heaven, only love remains. Our faith gives way to sight; our sin and sorrow burned away. Hope is actualized in his presence. May the love of God consume your heart, mind and soul; for when we die in thirst, full of desire for the Father, we pass from life to life. The power of God's love relativizes both life and death! Our pilgrimage and journey through the wilderness will one day come to an end. It is in this great desert that we come to discover just how thirsty we truly are. Let us never settle for the counterfeit offerings of the world that attempt to shrink our heart's desire. Like Christ himself, may we die of thirst.

"To the thirsty I will give water without price from the fountain of the water of life. He who conquers shall have this heritage, and I will be his God and he shall be my son" (Revelations 21:6-7).

PARADISUS DEI

Made in the USA
Columbia, SC
03 February 2019